About the Authors

Patricia Kelleher (PhD) and **Carmel Kelleher** (M Soc Sc.), sociologists, established Kelleher Associates in 1987. The firm specialises in the areas of evaluation research, poverty and social exclusion, women's issues, community consultation and local planning, the relationship between the state and voluntary organisations and rural development. It has extensive experience working jointly with the voluntary and statutory sectors in developing inter-agency policies and strategies. Kelleher Associates undertakes commissions for universities, government departments, private organisations, voluntary groups and the European Commission.

Maria Corbett, social policy analyst, undertook post-graduate work at the National College of Ireland, Maynooth and McMaster University in Canada, and has worked on many assignments with Kelleher Associates.

LEFT OUT ON THEIR OWN

Young People Leaving Care in Ireland

Patricia Kelleher
Carmel Kelleher
Maria Corbett

Oak Tree Press
Dublin
in association with
Focus Ireland

Oak Tree Press
Merrion Building
Lower Merrion Street
Dublin 2, Ireland
www.oaktreepress.com

A catalogue record of this book is
available from the British Library.

ISBN 1 86076 193-3

Cover Photograph by Derek Speirs.

Printed in the Republic of Ireland
by Colour Books Ltd.

Focus Ireland

Consultative Research Committee

Orla Barry, Focus Ireland
Michael Bruton*, Focus Ireland
Rachel Collier**, Focus Ireland
Mary Collins, Irish Foster Care Association
Siobhán Connolly, Out-of-Hours Service, Eastern Health Board
Patrick Donnelly/ Nuala Doherty, North-Eastern Health Board
Pauline Faughnan***, Social Science Research Centre
Noel Howard, Irish Association of Care Workers
Declan Jones, Focus Ireland, Chairperson
Sr. Stanislaus Kennedy, Focus Ireland
Eileen Keogh/ Bernadette McDonnell, Department of Health and Children
Liam Kilroy, Special Education Section Department of Education
Liam Lynch, Resident Managers Association
Frank Mulville, Focus Ireland
Justin O' Brien, Focus Ireland
Patricia O'Hara, Focus Ireland
Val O'Kelly, Acting Child Care Development Officer, North-Western
    Health Board
Fr. Joe O'Reilly, St. Joseph's School, Clonmel
Martin Tansey, Principal Probation Officer, Probation and Welfare
    Service

*   Resigned from Focus Ireland June 1999
**   Resigned from Focus Ireland January 1998
*** Resigned from Committee 1999

Covenant Status Research Committee

Kevin Brabazon, Chairman, Eason & Son Limited
Clive W Brownlee, Personnel Director, Guinness Ireland Group
Michael Bruton, Chief Executive, Focus Ireland
Damian Hannan, Research Professor, ESRI
Sr. Stanislaus Kennedy, President, Focus Ireland
Ciaran McCullagh, Department of Sociology, UCC
John Pinkerton, Centre Childcare Research, Queen's University
Valerie Richardson, Department of Sociology & Social Work, UCD
Mike Stein, Department of Social Policy and Social Work, UCD
Hilary Tovey, Sociology Department, Trinity College Dublin
Conor Ward, Emeritus Professor, St. Brigids

Contents

List of Tables

Acknowledgments

Many people assisted with this study and a warm thank you is extended to:

The staff of special schools for young offenders (funded by the Department of Education and Science) for giving generously of their time in tracking young people who had left their care. The staff of the Probation and Welfare Service Hostels (funded by the Department of Justice, Equality and Law Reform) and the personnel of the Eastern, North Eastern and the North-Western Health Boards who gave generously of their time in filling out monitoring forms and discussing issues concerning the young people leaving their care.

The Irish Foster Care Association (IFCA) which facilitated the research in many ways.

Residential care workers and workers in aftercare projects who supported the project.

Sinéad Hyland, Imelda O'Sullivan, Audrey Doyle and Michelle Kelleher who helped with the research.

Frank Mulville for making his expertise available to the researchers and helping in many ways, including organising group discussions on the issues arising in the research.

Trutz Haase, Jonathan Pratschke and Miriam Galvin for their expertise and undertaking data analysis.

Mike Stein, University of York, and John Pinkerton, Queen's University Belfast, who pioneered the methodology for research on young people leaving care. Our theoretical and practical understanding of the issues arising for young people leaving care was greatly enhanced as a result of discussions with Mike and John.

Pauline Faughnan, of the Social Science Research Centre, for her valuable comments.

Siobhán Parkinson for her assistance editing the report.

Patricia O'Hara, Damian Hannan, Justin O' Brien, Kathleen Maher, Cathleen O'Neill, Glenda Cimino and Roisin Conroy for their helpful comments.

The Consultative Committee for their constructive criticism and advice.

The community workers and activists in Ballymun Women's Resource Group, the SAOL project and Neighbourhood Youth Project in the north inner city of Dublin and the 'Clondalkin Youth and Support and Training Unit for sharing their insights with us.

John Lonergan, Governor of Mountjoy Prison.

The Eastern Health Board, the North-Eastern Health Board, the North-Western Health Board, the Department of Education and Science and the Probation and Welfare Service for providing the financial assistance for this study.

Claire Mulville, Martin Murphy, Hilary Little and Frank Houghton of Focus Ireland, who assisted with the administration of the research.

Sr. Stanislaus Kennedy, Rachel Collier, Michael Bruton, Orla Barry and Pauline Costello of Focus Ireland who ensured that the supports needed for the research were in place.

The Child Care Policy Unit at the Department of Health and Children, for providing funding for the publishing, design and promotion of this research.

The young people for sharing their experience of being in care and leaving care and to whom we owe a special debt of gratitude. We hope this research will contribute to the provision of improved supports and services for them.

Patricia Kelleher, PhD
Carmel Kelleher, M Soc Sc
Maria Corbett, M A
September 2000

Preface

This report identifies serious deficiencies in the provision for children in the care of the state in Ireland. It makes painful reading for policy makers and practitioners. The challenge for all of us is to face these hard realities and endeavour to address them.

Focus Ireland's consistent experience in its 15 years has been that young people presenting as homeless have very often been brought up in care or spent some time in the care of the state. This research now confirms that experience: one-third of the young people leaving the care of the health boards and over half of those leaving special schools for young offenders experience episodes of homelessness or spend time in detention centres at some stage during their first six months. By the time they have been two years out of care, the situation has deteriorated even further: a quarter of the young people leaving health board care have been in detention centres and two-thirds of them have experienced homelessness, while two-thirds of those leaving special schools have been in detention centres and a third have been homeless.

The reasons for this appalling situation are obvious. All young people find the process of transition from adolescence to adulthood, which includes leaving home, complex and difficult, but most of them have the support and encouragement of their families. Young people leaving care are very often cut off from or have poor relationships with their families, and there are no alternative formal support mechanisms in place to ease their transition into adult life. Furthermore, they often leave care abruptly and without preparation; yet are expected to achieve instant maturity and be able to live independently at an early age without support. It is hardly surprising that they find it extremely difficult to make a successful transition.

Anyone reading this report is inexorably driven to the conclusion that our childcare system is not working in the interest of children; that the state is not fulfilling its responsibility for the children in its care; and that the human rights of children are being violated on a daily basis in this country.

The root of the problem is lack of strategic planning and lack of a single vision and policy for childcare in this country. As long ago as 1970, the Kennedy Report recommended that the administrative responsibility for all aspects of childcare be transferred to the Department of Health, while responsibility for education should remain with the Department of Education and Science. This crucial recommendation was never implemented and the result is the uncoordinated response to children in need of care that we see today. We continue to have three government departments involved in childcare; and although one minister of state has responsibility for the co-ordination of these departments, we still have an unintegrated system that lacks coherence. Minister Frank Fahey and Minister Mary Hanafin have commendably attempted to involve all the departments in trying to draw up a national childcare strategy. However, if it does not lead to the establishment of one government department with responsibility for all aspects of childcare, the needs of our children will not be met. As long as this absurd situation continues we will have the fragmented and inadequate childcare service that we have today, which is so clearly shown to be failing in this report.

The Kennedy Report also clearly called for an aftercare policy for children leaving care, but 30 years later this research discovers the total absence of an aftercare system. Effective planning and development of childcare services is impossible without accurate data on young people in care and young people leaving care, but this report found an astonishing lack of basic information on young people in care and leaving care, including the total absence of a tracking mechanism for the follow-up of young people after they leave care. The current situation in the provision of aftercare for children leaving care is just short of grossly irresponsible.

The study also finds that children are being inappropriately placed, with many young people being allocated places not on the basis of need but on the basis of places available. And these are the children who *are* taken into care: many who need care remain outside the system for lack of resources. It is a national disgrace that children with care orders (i.e. children who are officially in the care of the state) are allowed to drift in and out of homelessness, sometimes involving sleeping on the streets, while others are inappropriately placed in psychiatric hospitals, in detention centres, prisons and hospitals.

Neither the young people in care nor their parents are adequately supported. Young people may be placed at a distance from their families, making contact difficult to maintain, while the parents are not supported to develop their parenting skills. Nor are parents given sufficient opportunity to participate in reviews and case conferences and decisions regarding the future of their children. While parents are often excluded, foster parents and childcare workers are also often unsupported and inadequately trained and demoralised by working in a system that is so manifestly failing.

A key principle of the Convention on the Rights of the Child (adopted by the UN in 1989 and signed by the Irish government in 1992) is that services and responses to children should be developed "in the best interest of the child". Our childcare system is clearly in contravention of that principle and thus violates the rights of children, and Focus Ireland calls for this violation to be recognised, addressed and reversed. Continuing to provide incremental change, as we have done in the past, will not combat the ad hoc-ery and lack of coherence that we experience daily in our childcare system. What we need now is an integrated response, under one properly resourced government department, working within a strategic national plan for services for children. The establishment of a highly skilled, professional and well-resourced inspectorate, with a wider remit and better resources than are currently the case, is vital for the proper regulation of our childcare system if the rights of our children are to be protected. Focus Ireland also calls for putting in place immediately an ombudsman to safeguard the rights of children.

Much of the debate around the provision for children in the care of the state has centred on the inadequacies and abuses of the past. In the past society could claim that it was not aware of the poor provision, the abuse and the violation of human rights, this is not the case today. This research confirms the serious deficiencies in the system we provide for our children who are in the care of the state.

Urgent action is required in Ireland if the rights of children and young people are to be realised. What we need now is vision and leadership and a response to the needs of children that respects and protects their welfare and rights.

Sr. Stanislaus Kennedy
President, Focus Ireland

1

Executive Summary and Recommendations

"When you are taken into care, you lose contact with the people you know and the area you know. When you leave care, you feel empty. You have no connections. You feel embarrassed. You don't know how to relate to the people around you or the place." — Young person, aged 17 years

A significant number of young people are being taken out of the "care" of their families and placed in the "care" of the state. This research raises questions as to whether putting young people in the care of the state gives them a better chance of growing up and developing a positive self-worth and identity. The study highlights that young people leaving care end up as nobody's responsibility. A large proportion are institutionalised or abandoned and unable to create, as young adults and future parents, what they may have never experienced themselves: a stable, secure and loving home, with long-term positive and caring relationships.

When young people fail to attend school or commit a prisonable offence, they may be placed by the courts in reformatory or industrial schools, known as special schools for young offenders, which are under the aegis of the Department of Education and Science.[1] The health boards under a care order may

---

[1] There are three reformatory schools and two industrial schools in Ireland. Two of the three reformatory schools and the two industrial schools cater for boys, while one reformatory school caters for girls. Young people are also

remove young people either voluntarily or compulsorily from the custody of their parents and place them in *foster* or *residential care*. In these circumstances, parents are considered to have failed in their parental duty towards the young person. Failure is seen to result from such factors as neglect, being unable to cope and the presence of abuse or suspected abuse in the home. The courts, prisons and special schools may also place young people in *probation hostels*, under the aegis of the Probation and Welfare Service.

Many of these children who are taken into the care of the state are born into a situation of poverty and social disadvantage. At an early age many children experience great emotional trauma because of violence in the home, sexual abuse, alcohol or drug addiction in the home, and/or loss of a parent through separation or death. Some of them, in addition, have special needs such as physical or mental disability. It is not surprising that such emotionally and socially traumatised children carry enormous unresolved grief, low self-worth, and anger. As a result, many of them exhibit disruptive behaviour, are irregular school attenders, misuse drugs and alcohol and/or become involved in crime.

The state does not have an adequate system for supporting families in crisis. Lower-income families, lacking such supports, are more likely to come to the attention of the gardai and social work services than their middle or upper-class counterparts who are better placed to finance the supports needed in a situation of family crisis or breakdown. Many children are taken into care when situational factors, such as family illness or crisis, combine with structural inequalities such as poverty, unemployment, and lack of housing.

Being in care can cause further disruption and instability in children's lives. They can feel stigmatised for being in care and not living in a "normal" family environment. Young people in long-term health board care may lack a basic knowledge of

---

placed in the two industrial schools by health boards under a voluntary care order, agreed between the family and health board. Industrial and reformatory schools are referred to as special schools for young offenders. Hence, these schools are referred to in the text as special schools.

their family background. Separation from parents and siblings for young people in care can cause enormous hurt, grief, shame and anger. Multiple admissions to care, multiple placements while in care, and inappropriate placements can undermine their already fragile sense of their own identity. When placements break down, the young person is often made to feel that it is his or her own fault, and this can result in an increased sense of insecurity and anxiety.

This study examines what happens to young people who leave state care and surveys their circumstances six months after leaving care and again two years later. The majority of young people leaving state care fail to make successful transitions from care. They are "left out on their own" to manage the difficult transitional period to adulthood. Many end up homeless or in prison. A range of recommendations are outlined which emerged from the collective experiences of those directly concerned with service provision. These recommendations must be implemented as a matter of urgency.

Why this Study was Commissioned

Many homeless young people who had been in the care of the state came to the attention of Focus Ireland services. It was important to find out what happens to young people on leaving care and after they leave care. Thus Focus Ireland made a decision to carry out a longitudinal study on young care leavers.

1.1 BACKGROUND TO STUDY

This is the first national study of young people leaving care in Ireland.[2] The overall aim of the study is to provide baseline information on young people leaving state care. The main aims are to:

---

[2] The study uses a well-developed methodology. Where possible the outcomes for care leavers are compared to the outcomes for the general population and to the results of the Northern Ireland study and the study undertaken in Britain. The study builds on the methodologies developed by the Leeds University Leaving Care Research Project (LLCRP) which was published in 1992 (Biehal, Clayden, Stein and Wade), and the leaving care study carried out in Northern Ireland by Pinkerton and McCrea (1996).

- Describe the background and recent developments in the foster care and residential care system in Ireland.

- Carry out three separate surveys of young people leaving care in order to monitor the circumstances of care-leavers six months and again two years after leaving care. The main research tool used is a Monitoring Form which was filled out by social workers and care staff.

- Undertake intensive interviews with 30 care leavers and to construct 70 case histories of young care-leavers based on information from the monitoring survey, from social workers and residential care workers, and from interviews with the young people themselves.

- Analyse leaving-care policy and practice based on the monitoring survey, documentary material, focus group discussions with social workers, staff from special schools, residential child care centres and aftercare services, discussions with staff of Traveller Families Care (an organisation for Travellers in care), discussions with members of the Irish Association of Young People in Care, members of the Irish Foster Care Association and discussions with groups concerned with youth at risk in three Dublin communities.

During the course of the study, it was observed that a large number of young people were homeless and were moving in and out of care. These young people were seeking accommodation and help from the Crisis Intervention Service of the Eastern Health Board ("out-of-hours service"). Focus Ireland, which commissioned the research, was of the opinion that this service should be included in the research. In order to get an understanding of the out-of-hours service, the researchers undertook a one-week survey of the numbers, characteristics and presenting problems of young people seeking the assistance of this service. This was updated two years later.

Research Population

The research population is comprised of three sub-groupings. It includes:

- Young people leaving the care of the country's five special schools for young offenders which are the responsibility of the Department of Education and Science. Of the population of 103 who left care, 90 per cent (93) were tracked six months after leaving care and 88 per cent (91) two years after leaving care.

- Young people leaving the care of three health board regions (the Eastern, North-Eastern and the North-Western). These regions were selected in order to get an overview of the circumstances of young people from a range of geographical backgrounds. Of the population of 56 young people, 87 per cent (49) were tracked six months after leaving care and 79 per cent (44) two years after leaving care.

- Young people leaving the care of the two Dublin probation hostels, which are the responsibility of the Department of Justice, Equality and Law Reform. All six young people leaving the care of the Probation and Welfare Service were tracked six months later. None of these six young people, however, was tracked two years later. This was, in part, due to the change of staff in the Probation and Welfare Service responsible for probation hostels.

The study populations are outlined in Table 1.1 below.

Table 1.1: Numbers of Young People in the Leaving Care Study Population

Type of Care	Leaving Care	Surveyed Six Months On	Surveyed Two Years On
Special school	103	93	91
Health board	56	49	44
Probation and Welfare Service	6	6	0
Total	165	148	135

1.2 MAIN RESEARCH FINDINGS

Social Disadvantage

The vast majority of care leavers come from a background of poverty and social disadvantage.[3]

Approximately 25 per cent of the study population had a parent who was in full-time employment. This was at a time when there was a national unemployment rate of 10 per cent (Davy Economic Research 1997).

The special school population was ten times more likely than the general population, to live in local authority housing, and the health board leaving care population was eight times more likely than the general population to live in local authority housing.

Young people with a Traveller background made up 9 per cent of the health board population and 12 per cent of the special school population. The Traveller community makes up 0.4 per cent of the population nationally. No other ethnic minorities were identified in the leaving care populations.

On average care leavers leave school at an early age and with a low level of education qualifications. Fifty-five per cent of the health board care-leavers, and 44 per cent of special schools care leavers, left school without any qualifications. This compares to 4 per cent of the general population who left school without any qualifications (Williams and Collins, 1997).

Only 1 per cent of the special school population and 10 per cent of the health board population had sat for the Leaving Certificate examination. This contrasts with 82 per cent of school-leavers in the general population, at the time of the study, who sat for the Leaving Certificate.

---

[3] As stated in the main body of this study, this is not to imply that parents from lower-income families are less able to provide or less capable of looking after their children than middle or upper-middle class families. Rather, the perspective of the study is that many children are taken into care when structural inequalities such as poverty, unemployment or lack of housing combine with situational factors such as illness and family breakdown. Also, middle and upper-income families are less likely to come under the surveillance of the state.

Six months after leaving care, less than a quarter of the health board population and only 15 per cent of the special school population was at work. This was at a time when the national unemployment rate in Ireland was 10 per cent.

Two years later, as Table 1.2 indicates, there was some increase in the percentage of young people at work for both populations. This reflects the buoyancy of the economy in recent years. However, young people who were at work were in low-paid employment. As this study reveals, many of the young people have low educational achievements. The challenge is to support young people to remain in employment and to encourage them to increase their educational and vocational skills in order that they can avail of enhanced labour market opportunities.

Table 1.2: *Work and Educational Achievements*

Education and Work Achievements	Special School Population	Health Board Population
Sat the Leaving Certificate	1%	10%
At Work Six Months On	15%	24%
At Work Two Years On	20%	34%

Emotional Trauma

Many young people in care experience great emotional trauma resulting from such factors as violence in the home, sexual abuse, alcohol and drug addiction in the home and loss of a parent through separation or death.

Table 1.3 summarises some of the difficulties experienced by young people in the study populations.

Table 1.3: *Percentage of Young People with Difficulties*

Difficulties	Special School Population	Health Board Population
Experienced childhood sexual abuse	18%	41%
Domestic violence in family	49%	40%
Had a special need	23%	39%

Forty-one per cent of the health board population were identified as having been sexually abused. This was twice as high as
the reported figure for the special school population.

Domestic violence also featured significantly in the lives of
care leavers with 49 per cent of special school leavers and 40
per cent of the health board care leavers having experienced
violence in the home. This contrasts with a national incidence of
domestic violence of 18 per cent (Kelleher, Kelleher and
O'Connor, 1995).

For both the special school and the health board care leavers, there was a significant group of young people with a special need. ***Almost one-quarter of the special school leavers
and two-fifths of the health board care leavers had a special
need.*** Special need was defined in terms of a physical disability, learning disability, i.e. mental handicap, and mental health
difficulty such as clinical depression, eating disorder, suicidal
tendencies and propensity to inflict self-harm. The percentage
of young people with a special need was much greater than in
the study in England by Biehal *et al.,* 1992, which found that 12
per cent of the population had special needs.

***As a result of the emotional trauma they have experi-
enced, young people leaving care carry enormous unresolved grief and loss. It is not surprising that many of them
exhibit a range of difficulties, detailed in the report, such as
disruptive behaviour, delayed learning, irregular school
attendance, drug and alcohol abuse and involvement in
crime.***

Care History and Placements

Thirty-one per cent of the health board population had five or
more placements and 40 per cent of the special school population had three or more placements. In addition, the frequent
change-over of social workers and care staff further threatens
their sense of security and wellbeing. One young person
stated:

> "I moved from one residential home to another. I found it
> really hard. There were new staff and new surroundings.
> There were also different rules."

Young people in health board care tended to be in care for longer periods than the special school population. Eighty-four per cent of the health board care leavers and 89 per cent of special school leavers had spent more than one year in care. Eleven per cent of special school leavers and just over half of health board care leavers had been in care for more than five years.

Twenty-five per cent of the special school population had been in health board care and 7 per cent of the health board population had been in special schools.

Inappropriate Placements

Twenty-five per cent[4] of all young people in the study population were considered to be inappropriately placed in the care system. The study found that many young people are allocated places not on the basis of need but on the basis of places available. Examples of misplacement are provided throughout the main body of the report. Young people were misplaced in the health board system primarily because health boards had not sufficient placements to respond to the therapeutic and drug treatment needs of young people.

Young people were placed in special schools when their real need was for short-stay specialised drug treatment services or therapeutic services to respond to severe trauma resulting from childhood sexual abuse or family conflict. Other young people needed residential services to respond to the specific challenges of mental handicap. Homelessness and family breakdown were other key issues facing the young people.

The following cases are examples of inappropriate placements:

> *Stephen* was committed to a secure detention centre (special school) for breaking his mother's window. Staff were of the opinion that the underlying issue was one of family breakdown. His mother was in a new relationship and had two young children with her new partner. Stephen felt left

---

[4] One-third of health board population were misplaced and 23 per cent of the special school population were misplaced.

out of the new family and began to react against his mother. His mother felt that he was out of control and asked the court that he be taken into a secure unit. The school subsequently found it difficult to engage his mother in a process to resolve the difficulties between her and Stephen. Staff are of the opinion that Stephen should not be detained in a secure unit. His underlying problem is the need to resolve the problems with his mother.

Eoin has a mild mental handicap and has difficulties with learning. At the age of 13, the courts committed him to a detention centre (special school) for school non-attendance. While in the special school he found it difficult to interact with such a large group of boys and had difficulty following staff directions and rules. Staff are of the opinion that a smaller unit which could accommodate a person with mild mental handicap and learning difficulties would have been a more suitable placement.

Inappropriate placements are linked to the absence of appropriate places being available and the lack of a centralised assessment and placement unit at regional health board level or a centralised placement system for special schools. The practice of misplacing young people raises important human rights issues. The practice of detaining a young person in a special school when it is not necessary can cause severe anger and resentment as the young person's personal movements and liberties are needlessly and unnecessarily restricted. Also, it is not cost effective.

Placement Breakdown

This study found that for 55 per cent of young people who left health board care, their leaving care was precipitated by a crisis with the placement breaking down or the young person walking out of the placement. Nearly 30 per cent of young people who left the care of special schools either absconded, were returned to other special schools or sent to a place of detention.

Many placements break down because the placement, in the first instance, is not appropriate to meet the needs of the young person. This is often the result of the limited choice available when the young person is being placed. Despite this, the young person is often made to feel that it is her or his fault when the placement breaks down. A variety of other factors, such as personal identity issues, unresolved anger and a search for increased autonomy, can also cause placements to break down. When a placement breaks down, the transition from care, by definition, is not planned and the young person is often left isolated and alone with an increased sense of insecurity and anxiety.

Ambivalent Relationship to Birth Families

Even though many care leavers feel ambiguous about their care placement, they are also ambivalent about returning home. Young people leaving care experience high levels of personal distress as past experiences within the family are re-membered. Many feel that they are not welcome at home and some have difficulty readjusting to family and neighbourhood life. They experience a lack of familiarity with routine and so-cial networks, which other young people take for granted.

In turn, birth families, and in particular mothers, feel stigma-tised when their children are taken into care. They can feel that they are being labelled as a "bad mother" and tend to view health board intervention as a form of surveillance and control, whose primary responsibility is to protect children, and very little support is offered to families who have children taken into care. Mothers can feel embarrassment and shame about ac-knowledging that their children are in care and about visiting their children in care (O'Higgins, 1996). There is therefore a need to support mothers and families who have young people in care.

Support and State Policy

Residential care workers, social workers and foster-carers make significant responses to the needs of young people while they are in care. Key relationships are developed and intensive support is provided to the young person over an extended pe-riod of time.

However, special schools have no legislative basis for providing aftercare. As one key worker in a special school explained:

> "You help them to pack their bags, take the posters down from the wall and say goodbye. You tell them to keep in contact and to ring you."

Health boards may provide aftercare under Section 45 of the *Child Care Act, 1991.* **The Department of Health and Children, however, has no written policy on aftercare and aftercare is at the discretion of Social Work Managers at Community Care Area level. Many foster families provide aftercare for young care leavers in their own time and from their own resources.** Leaving care for many young people can mean anxiety, fear and loneliness, as one young person explained:

> "The eighteenth birthday is huge for us. While others are looking forward to their eighteenth birthday, I dreaded it. There are big emotions around it. You don't know what the next step is going to be. When I turned eighteen I knew that that was it. Most social workers don't keep people on. I often thought that I would have been better off putting up with the beatings at home."

The vast majority of care leavers had little or no support from statutory agencies two years after leaving care. Twenty-seven per cent of health board care leavers had contact with the social work service.

Only 15 per cent of young people who left special schools had contact with social workers. This contact was for the most part the result of the social worker having contact with the family on issues relating to child protection. Contact with the Probation and Welfare Service was significant, with 62 per cent having contact six months after leaving care and 40 per cent having contact two years after leaving care.

Other supports came from voluntary agencies (16 per cent), residential units (7 per cent) and special youth projects (5 per cent).

Despite the fact that 75 per cent of the health board leavers and 67 per cent of special school care leavers had difficulties with their families, many care leavers have a strong desire to live in a "family" environment and to have their relationships with their family "normalised". Two years after leaving care 75 per cent of health board care leavers had contact with a family member. However, in less than one-third of all families was the relationship between the young person and the family perceived by social workers and care staff to be frequent and satisfactory.

Sixty per cent of the special school leavers had contact with a family member two years after leaving care. The relationship was perceived by care workers to be frequent and satisfactory for only 47 per cent of young people.

Out-of-Hours Service

This study found that the objectives of the out-of-hours service (crisis intervention service), which is to link young people out-of-home back into mainstream Community Care services, are not being met. A core group of young people are drifting in and out of homelessness and their long-term needs are not being addressed. The main problem is that there are not a sufficient number of appropriate placements and support services for adolescents available at local Community Care Area level. This has put pressure on the out-of-hours service. The service, which was established as an emergency service in the city centre, has become a mainstream service for young homeless people.

This study found that there are some children with care orders who, due to insufficient places, end up sleeping on the streets and drifting in and out of homelessness. Community Care Teams and the crisis intervention services (out-of-hours service) of the Eastern Health Board are not dealing adequately with the problems of such young people, who may or may not get a bed for the night on approaching the crisis services. Sleeping rough can further expose these children to dangers of prostitution and drug abuse.

Current practice raises the question of how Section 5 of the *Child Care Act 1991,* which deals with the accommodation rights of young people who are out of home, should be interpreted. Given the ambiguity of Section 5, it is incumbent now on the Minister for Health and Children to clarify and define a policy in relation to the eligibility of homeless children to accommodation and support services.

Difficulties Two Years On

Two years after leaving care, the lives of many care leavers in the study were characterised by despair, hopelessness and chronic social instability. Staff and social workers estimated that 59 per cent of the health board population, and 76 per cent of the special school population, needed additional services such as supported accommodation, addiction treatment, counselling and intensive probation supervision.

Accommodation

Almost half of the health board population had difficulties with accommodation six months after leaving care, and over a quarter had difficulties two years later. Thirty-two per cent of the special school population had difficulties with accommodation six months after leaving care and 30 per cent still had difficulties two years after leaving care.

Table 1.4: Difficulties Two Years On

Difficulties	Health Board	Special Schools
Accommodation	27%	30%
Addiction	30%	43%
Childhood Sexual Abuse	23%	12%
Prostitution	14%	3%

Addiction, Childhood Sexual Abuse and Prostitution

Two years after leaving care, 43 per cent of the special school population, and 30 per cent of the health board population, had problems with addiction. Unresolved problems surrounding childhood sexual abuse affected almost one-quarter of the health board population. Two years after leaving care 14 per cent of the health board population and 3 per cent of the special schools population were suspected of being involved in prostitution.

Alcohol abuse and drug-taking is often used to kill the pain and the experience of the past, as the following example illustrates:

> "My father, who is now in prison for abusing another young person, sexually abused me. I used to shower ten times a day. I felt dirty and too embarrassed to tell anyone. When I took heroin it took away the feelings, which were coming over my body, I wouldn't even tell the psychologist who I was seeing what was really wrong with me."

Homelessness

Six months after leaving care, 33 per cent of the health board population had experienced homelessness, and 30 per cent of the special school population had experienced homelessness. This is 10 per cent higher than was evident in the Northern Ireland (Pinkerton and McCrea, 1996) and England (Biehal *et al.*, 1992) studies where 20 per cent of the leaving care population in both studies experienced homelessness.

Two years after leaving care 68 per cent of the health board population, and 33 per cent of the special school population, had experienced homelessness.

Prison

Thirty-nine per cent of young people who left the care of special schools were either in a place of detention, or had been in a place of detention, during the six months after leaving care. *Two years after leaving care 65 per cent of the special school population had been in a place of detention or prison. During these two years many young people had been in a place of detention a number of times.*

A search was undertaken of prison records at the end of 1999, which for some young people was three years after leaving care. The search revealed that 63 per cent (65 young people) of the total population of 103 young people had been in prison or in a place of detention. A further three young people had been returned to a special school. This means that 66 per cent (68 individuals) of the special school population had been to either a special school or place of detention or adult prison since leaving care.

The percentage of young people in the health board population who had been sentenced to prison increased from 10 per cent six months after leaving care, to 25 per cent two years later.

Table 1.5 shows the percentage of young people in the survey population who had been in detention or who had been homeless in the two-year period after leaving care.

Table 1.5: Two Years After Leaving Care

Population	% Who had been in Detention	% Who had been Homeless	Numbers Tracked Two Years After Leaving Care
Special school population	65%	33%	91
Health Board population	25%	68%	44

Transition from Care

Logistic regression analysis was undertaken on the survey data in order to ascertain the factors related to the young person making a successful transition from care (See Appendix 3). A successful transition was predicted by the young person not being arrested, the young person not being committed to prison or the young person entering stable employment. Using these independent variables, a binary response model was used which calculated the propensity of care leavers to succeed or fail in the transition from care.

Young people who made successful transitions from care were less likely to be abusing drugs and alcohol or to have been victims of sexual abuse. They were more likely to have a stable care placement, fewer placement moves while in care and a planned transition from care, which was not precipitated by a placement breakdown. They were also

more likely to have consistent and stable support from a family member or from their foster family.

Specific results of the analysis are summarised below.

Arrests

The probability of a young person being arrested is related to whether or not the young person abuses drugs, is male, and whether or not the young person has a stable care placement: Young people who were arrested were:

- Five times more likely to be abusing alcohol.

- Three times more likely to be abusing drugs.

- Six times more likely to be male as female.

- Eighteen times more likely to have had a breakdown of their transition placement or to have absconded from a special school. The likelihood of being arrested after leaving care increases by a factor of one and a half for each move from one care placement to another.

- Twenty-three times more likely to have attended a special school as opposed to being in health board care.

Prison

The probability of a care leaver being committed to prison is related to whether or not the young person abuses drugs. A young care leaver committed to prison is three times more likely to be abusing drugs than a young person not committed to prison.

Employment and Unemployment

- Young care leavers who took up stable employment were more than twice as likely to have received support from a statutory agency or to have received formal preparation on leaving care.

- Young people not abusing drugs were six to seven times more likely to be in employment and young people who were unemployed were four times more likely to be abusing drugs.

- Young people leaving care, with a history of sexual abuse, were three times more likely to be unemployed.

Convention on the Rights of the Child

At an international level the *Convention on the Rights of the Child,* adopted by the United Nations in 1989 and signed by the Irish government in 1992, is a landmark in international human rights legislation. The Convention has positioned children at the forefront of the worldwide movement for human rights. The key principle on which the Convention is based is that services and responses to children should be developed "in the best interests of the child".

In the absence of facilities and appropriate services, children in Ireland are resorting to the high court to have their rights enforced. Newspapers contain on a regular basis judicial statements from irritated high court judges berating the incompetence of government departments and agencies for not responding to the needs of children and young people. In the absence of appropriate services, children who are not psychiatrically ill are being incarcerated in adult psychiatric hospitals. Children, who have not committed a crime, are being held in detention centres and adult prisons, and children under 12 years of age who are homeless are being retained in hospitals as "social admissions".[5] Children are also being sent out of the country to be cared for.

Despite the fact that these cases receive regular publicity from the media, there is little public dissent and the rights of children and young people are not being respected.

---

[5] In 1998, 86 children were placed in five Dublin hospitals. The average length of stay in any one hospital for these children ranged from one night to 52 nights. This by any standards constitutes neglect on the part of the state and a severe infringement of the rights of children. Hospital settings are inappropriate environments in which to meet the emotional and psychological needs of these children.

1.3 RECOMMENDATIONS

Failings

This study documents major failings in the child care system. These include:

- No guidelines, policy or designated budget for aftercare and resettlement

- Lack of appropriate accommodation options for young people who leave care

- Lack of community-based services for adolescents at risk

- Insufficient care placements for adolescents requiring care

- Inappropriate placements, including the practice of placing young people who have not committed a crime, in industrial schools

- The fact that leaving care is precipitated by a placement breakdown in a large proportion of cases

- The fact that large numbers of young people have multiple care placements while in care, which creates a destabilising environment for the young people

- Failure of the out-of-hours service to meet its objectives with some young people, who access the service, being left to sleep rough on the streets

- Absence of an emergency service for young people under 12 years who are placed as "social admissions" in hospitals

- Inadequate data base on young people in care and on leaving care.

The main recommendations relate to the three following areas:

- Leaving care policy and practice

- Community-based services for adolescents

- Reform of the child care system.

These three recommendations are elaborated on below.

Leaving Care Policy

Leaving care policy and practice is weak. In this context there is a need for the Minister for Health and Children to issue a Ministerial Order, under the *Child Care Act, 1991*. *The order should require health boards to recognise that the process of becoming an adult takes time, and health boards should provide support and information to care leavers up until they reach 25 years if such support is requested. Care leavers should not be cut off abruptly from the support of social workers when they reach 18 years of age and they should have some control in the decision to end the relationship with the social work services.* Where young people move from one health board region to another, health boards should ensure that the relevant health board is informed and that the appropriate support is provided, where required.

The Department of Education and Science should provide a Ministerial Order, and if necessary new legislation to facilitate special schools to develop aftercare programmes.

The following issues relating to leaving care need to be addressed:

- All health boards and special schools should have a written and accessible aftercare policy, and government departments should provide a designated budget for this purpose. The policy should address the following needs of young people:

    ◊ Accommodation and entitlements to basic household items, on moving into new accommodation

    ◊ Finance

    ◊ Employment, training and education

    ◊ Mentoring

    ◊ Health

    ◊ Access to age therapeutic and counselling services.

- Given the vulnerability and the young age of both health board and special school leavers, a range of accommodation options should be available. There is need for:

  ◊ Priority access to local authority accommodation for young people over 18 who are leaving care

  ◊ Transitional housing where young people can experience living in a less institutionalised environment

  ◊ Affordable furnished flats

  ◊ Supported housing in local areas

  ◊ An increased number of probation hostels, and in particular probation hostels for females.

Where the young person moves to independent living, he or she should be supported to find accommodation and to move into, and settle in, accommodation. They should also be entitled to a moving-in allowance to cover designated household items. Aftercare policies should also address the role of foster families, residential care units and birth families in providing aftercare.

Foster Care

Foster care plays a central role in the care system. It is important that there are proper planning and reviews while the young person is in foster care.[6] This study found that there is a lot of ambiguity as to what constitutes a care plan and that, in some cases, care plans were not written down. Where care plans were written down there was not always the resources to address the issues raised in the care plan. Prior to the young person reaching 18 years of age, it is important that both the foster-carers, and foster children, are provided with real choices in relation to future plans for the young person. These and other issues need to be addressed:

---

[6] *The Child Care Regulations, 1995* published by the Department of Health set out procedures and guidelines for the preparation and review of care plans.

- There is a need for the care plan to specify whether or not the young person is to remain with the foster parents, return to his or her natural family, or move to independent living

- Many young people, when they reach 18 years and leave care, continue to be supported by their foster carers. This should be recognised and a befriending allowance to cover basic expenses should be provided

- Special provision should be made for young people with special needs, such as intellectual disability or mental health problems, who continue to live with their foster families after they reach the age of 18 years

- Special training is needed for foster carers to deal with adolescent crises and to respond to young people who exhibit challenging behaviour.

Residential Health Board Care

At present much of the outreach and aftercare work undertaken by key workers in residential care is carried out in their own time. In this context:

- All health board residential units should have a specific budget for outreach and resettlement work as part of an aftercare service

- Residential units should acknowledge that it is important for care leavers to maintain contact. Hence, staff of the units need to provide the opportunity for ex-residents, if they so wish, to visit residential units in their adult life

- Residential units also need to be resourced to work with the families of the young people in their care.

Birth Families

Natural parents need to be supported when children are taken into care. Parents need to be supported to develop their self-confidence, self-esteem and life-coping skills. They should be given the opportunity to participate effectively in review meetings and case conferences, and, in decisions regarding the future of their child in so far as this is compatible with the rights and best interests of the child.

Families, and mothers in particular, as consumers of the child care service, have not been given a voice as to how services should be structured and delivered. It is important that their views on services are documented and made known. Each health board, in conjunction with the Department of Education and Science and the Probation and Welfare Service, should fund:

- Peer group support networks for parents of young people in care

- A research project on the needs of mothers and families of young people taken into care.

Young Care Leavers

The principle of empowering young people underpins the Child Care Act, 1991, and the United Nations Convention on the Rights of the Child. In this context there is need to introduce a range of initiatives for young people to empower young people. These should include:

- Health boards and special school should recognise the right of young people to participate in making care plans and in review meetings. Young people need to be supported if participation is to be meaningful.

- Health board policies should also recognise the right of young people to make a complaint in relation to the aftercare services.

- Many young people leaving care in the Eastern Health Board Region end up accessing the out-of-hours service and living in supported lodgings. A count of young homeless people who use the out-of-hours service should be undertaken and their needs should be assessed. A resettlement and aftercare programme should be put in place.

- There is need for a prison release and support programme for young people coming out of prison.

- Health boards and organisations such as Focus Ireland and the Salvation Army that are providing services for young Travellers who are homeless should be encouraged to develop culturally appropriate responses to the needs of young Travellers. The out-of-hours service should have access to beds in residential centres specifically for Travellers or to residential centres where staff are trained to respond to the needs of Travellers.

- The Department of Education and Science and the Department of Health and Children should fund a leaving care support organisation with the following range of services:

  ◊ A drop-in centre

  ◊ Peer-group forums

  ◊ A newsletter for young people in care and young people leaving care

  ◊ An information and independent advocacy service to provide information on such issues as social welfare, training and work opportunities, accommodation, and help for young people to fill out forms and pursue their entitlements to legal rights

  ◊ Support young people in care or who have left care to search for their birth parents

  ◊ Informal support to help young people (both those who have left care and who are still in care) to cope with personal crises

  ◊ A mentoring service to provide personal support to young people and to assist them to develop and implement education and training plans.

An ombudsman for children should be appointed, as a matter of urgency, in order to assist young people to have their rights enforced.

Community-based Adolescent Services

The difficult personal issues that many older adolescents leaving care experience are evident from the study. In terms of policy responses, adolescents are a forgotten group and should now become the recipients of targeted state expenditure. Adolescents can be difficult to engage and can exhibit complex behavioural problems such as anger, violence and addiction. Many of these young people have been in multiple care placements where foster-carers and residential units have been unable to engage them and respond to their needs. They can also feel further stigmatised and marginalised by their negative experiences with statutory services.

The health boards should fund specialist adolescent teams, which would work with young people up to 25 years of age. They should target care leavers and young people leaving prison. They should also work with young people who are at risk of being taken into care.

These projects should be linked to a broader community-based, inter-agency approach, involving community-based training, education, work placement, drug treatment services, adventure sports projects, garda youth diversion projects and transitional housing accommodation. Young people who do not have appropriate family support should be linked to a mentoring programme, which would provide a local trained mentor to support the young person leaving care.[7] The programme should involve the development of individualised plans, a tracking system linked to financial incentives on achieving targets and support in carrying out plans.

Intensive Probation Supervision (IPS) programmes should form part of a network of community-based support services.[8] Intensive Probation Supervision programmes seek to divert offenders from prison. Group-based modules are used to challenge offending behaviour and challenge participants to reflect on factors related to their involvement in crime, such as addic-

---

[7] Mentoring programmes are being piloted in Dublin's north inner city for individuals who find it difficult to access mainstream services.

[8] The Bridge Project in Dublin and Grattan House in Cork have developed a model which could be adopted at community level.

tion, family relationships, violence and anger management. Intensive one-to-one contact, with key Probation Officers, provides ongoing support to participants.

The Departments of Health and Children, Education and Science, and, Justice, Equality and Law Reform should jointly fund these projects. Designated budgets specifically for adolescent programmes should be provided. Pilot projects in the Eastern Health Board region should be undertaken in Ballymun, Dublin's north inner city and Clondalkin in Dublin, and in Navan and Drogheda in the North Eastern Health Board region, where problems are most acute.[9]

Reform of the Child Care System

The care system should be radically reformed. The logic of two separate care systems, administered by separate government departments, one by the Department of Health and Children and a second by the Department of Education and Science, is called into question in this report. The misplacement of significant numbers of young people in care points to the urgent need for greater flexibility in reallocating places within that system. However, in the short term, since the political will to unify the two systems of care is not in evidence, at least a centralised system of allocations in each system is necessary.

Centralised Allocation System

A centralised allocations unit could maximise the use of care placements in the special schools. Young people should be allocated places on the basis of need, and not on

---

[9] The Eastern Health Board areas are suggested for the following reasons. The largest numbers of young people accessing the out-of-hours service are from Area 7, which comprises both the north inner city and Ballymun. Also, a community-based adolescent programme will need to link into the already existing infrastructure of services. Both of these areas have developed models, which an adolescent programme could link into. Clondalkin has already established a project for tracking young people who are marginalised from mainstream services (and which has been evaluated by Unique Perspectives [1999]. Drogheda is suggested as it has two adolescent units and an infrastructure of aftercare services is being developed there. Navan is the largest town in County Meath and has a concentration of disadvantaged youth.

the basis of places available. The detention of young people should be kept to a minimum, as detention deprives the young person of day-to-day responsibility for managing his or her own life.

The proposed centralised allocations and assessment unit should have a greater range of accommodation options than is at present available to special schools, such as locally based units, halfway houses, and group homes.

There are anomalies in the regional distribution of current care places in special schools. This results in many young people being placed in residential care long distances from their homes. Any new provision should attempt to redress this imbalance.

A centralised allocations unit is also needed in the Eastern Health Board. Tutt (1997) states that the present practice whereby the placement of young people in care is dispersed throughout the ten Community Care Areas is unproductive. It involves the duplication of work, as individual social workers search for places throughout the ten Community Care Areas. Tutt (1997) recommends the establishment of a centralised assessment unit, and this report endorses that recommendation.

Need for Accurate Data

This report found an absence of an adequate database on young people in the care of health boards and on leaving health board care. This was particularly evident in the Eastern Health Board region where social worker managers for the most part could not identify the leaving care population for the present study. Up-to-date accurate data on all young people in care and leaving the care of the state is essential for effective strategic planning and management of services. There is also a need for a mechanism to track the circumstances of young people after they leave care.

There should be a requirement on health boards to publish standardised statistics on young people in their care in their annual reports published under Section 8 of the *Child Care Act, 1991*. The lack of standardisation of data between health boards means that it is difficult to make comparisons in trends between health board regions and to monitor trends over time in any one health board region.

Policy on Special Schools

The function of special schools for young offenders is unclear, and policy relating to special schools is unclear. It vacillates between welfare and rehabilitation and punishment and restriction. In times of crisis media publicity, public opinion and political expediency influence policy. For example, during the course of the present study, a young person detained in a special school stole and burnt cars while on home leave. As a result of the publicity surrounding the case, home leave was severely curtailed for several months for all young people in the school. This measure impeded the implementation of care plans based on the young people's needs.

There is a need for a clear policy statement from the government on the function and role of special schools, and on the extent to which they are rehabilitative and educative. Given the trauma of many young people, who are referred to special schools, there is a need for schools to have access to a range of therapies that respond to specific traumas experienced by young care leavers.

Once a clear policy is stated, day-to-day practice in the special schools should be examined within the context of this policy.

Needs Assessment, Care Plans and Good Practice

In accordance with the *Child Care Ac, 1991*, health board social workers are required to develop care plans for young people in care. There is an ambiguity as to what constitutes a care plan. The research found that a proportion of health board care plans were not written down, and that the format of written care plans varied enormously.

In cases of long-term foster placements, there is a need for a structured plan which specifies whether or not the young person is to remain with the foster parents, return to her or his natural family or move to independent living.

Where a young person returns home, from either a foster placement or a residential care placement, the natural family should be supported to help the young person settle in with the family.

A large proportion of health board care leavers in the present study left because of a placement breakdown. Many of these breakdowns might have been prevented if social workers had more time and resources to carry through care plans and to anticipate an oncoming crisis.

There is a need for the Department of Health and Children to develop national guidelines on care plans. Professionals working with young people need access to ongoing training in needs assessment, and the development of care plans. They need to be facilitated to share experiences and models of good practice. Residential workers, who play a central role in the residential care system, need to be included in this process. There is also a need for post-care meetings between the young person, the residential care worker and the social worker. Resources need to be made available for this purpose.

Challenging Behaviour

There are increasing numbers of young people coming into the care system who exhibit difficult, challenging and sometimes dangerous behaviour. This is the result of extreme hurt, isolation or rejection. Therapeutic Crisis Intervention (TCI) is being used in some special schools and health boards as a response to aggressive behaviour.

There is a need to pilot different approaches to what works with these young people, and to exchange models of good practice between health board regions, and between health boards and schools. The model developed by the North-Western Health Board and outlined by Gogarty (1995) is an example of an approach that responds to the trauma and grief which young people experience and is seen by staff to be effective.

Placements for Specialised Needs

There is an urgent need for additional care placements, at local Community Care Area level, which can respond to the trauma and challenging behaviour and lifestyle of some adolescents. These care placements should include high-support units with a high level of staff and resources. They should also include foster care placements and community-based units, linked to local community networks and services such as counselling, drug treatment services, work and training.

Units need to be staffed by trained adolescent workers and foster-carers should be given specialist training in working with adolescents. Social workers, who are responsible for young people in these units, also need special training in work with adolescents. These projects need to be monitored and evaluated.

Projects providing short-term accommodation for young people need to be linked to a long-term accommodation strategy, which includes the private rented sector, social housing and local authority housing. It is only when this continuum of accommodation options are provided that the needs of young care leavers can be met.

Residential Care

The role and function of residential care is being transformed by the changing needs of children and young people. As a result of high court judgements, health boards are required to provide high-support and special care places, which will account for a substantial proportion of residential care provision. A defined policy and role for residential care needs to be established by the Department of Health and Children.

Many residential units are also undergoing a transition whereby control is being transferred from religious communities to state management. This period of transition can be stressful on staff. Residential care workers are undertaking complex work with adolescents. Their work is undervalued and their commitment to children and young people unacknowledged.

Residential care staff have to deal with an increasing number of young people who have difficulties with addiction and an increasing number of allegations of physical and sexual abuse. They regularly work in situations where even their most innocent remarks or normal displays of affection towards children are open to misinterpretation. There is an increasing sense that the remedies being put in place to redress abuses of the past are leading to practices that lack spontaneity and are clinically devoid of feeling. The result is a lowering of morale among residential care workers. Also, many residential units are finding it difficult to retain staff. The retention of staff is essential to the effective working of the child care system as young people need consistency in their relationship with staff. There is a need for:

- Ongoing training to enable staff to respond to the new demands placed on them

- Adequate professional supervision for staff

- Upgrading of staff positions

- The development of a career structure for child care workers

- Training and resources for residential units to engage with and support families who have children and young people taken into care.

A register of qualified care workers who are available for emergency cover should also be set up. In the absence of such a register, nurses are being employed to cover emergency situations. In the absence of sufficient numbers of trained people to deal with complex behavioural difficulties, security firms are being employed to deal with children who have complex and challenging behaviour.[10]

---

[10] "TD Critical of Arrangements for Children Needing Special Care", *Irish Times*, 1 January 2000.

Foster-Carers

Foster care is now established as the most important source of alternative family care. Several issues in relation to foster carers need to be addressed:

- The role foster-carers play in the child care system should be acknowledged and foster-carers need to be valued and to feel valued.

- The foster-care allowance should be increased in order to cover the expenses involved and to ensure that foster-carers are not out-of-pocket.

- An increased number of foster placements are breaking down when foster children reach their teens. Social workers need to be able to anticipate placement breakdown and make effective interventions. When placements break down, foster-carers need to be supported to deal with the crises.

- Increased resources need to be provided for the recruitment of foster-carers. The long delay in assessing applicants in some Community Care Areas is unsatisfactory.

- More training and information on the child should be available to foster-carers prior to the placement of the foster child. Additional resources should also be provided for in-service training on particular issues, for example on how to support birth parents, how to support one's own children, how to respond to aggressive behaviour and how to handle allegations of abuse. Special training is also needed for foster-carers willing to support adolescents who have special needs.

- Issues for foster-carers surrounding care plans and leaving care are outlined above in Section 1.3.

- A longitudinal research study should be undertaken on foster care to identify the factors which are conducive to successful care placements and the factors which lead to placement breakdowns.

1.4 CONCLUDING SUMMARY

In a broad sense the issue of children in care must be seen in the context of child poverty. Closing the gap between the rich and poor must become a priority as the impact of child care interventions is limited by the severe poverty experienced by many families who have children taken into care.

This study indicates that for many care leavers, their circumstances after leaving care are bleak. Two years on, the lives of many young people in the study were characterised by despair, hopelessness, and chronic social instability. Many are still displaced people, often left to manage the difficult transitional period between the ages of 18 to 25 on their own.

This study provides compelling evidence of the need to seriously rethink the supports needed by young people on leaving care and in particular on the need for an aftercare policy, which would lead to more successful outcomes for young people.

Vision and leadership have been absent and there is need for a broad response which fully respects and protects the rights and welfare of children and young people. Urgent action is required if children are to be protected as outlined in the *UN Convention on the Rights of the Child*.

The system's response to many young people is failing due to a lack of resources and an unwillingness to address the issue of the fragmented child care system, where the responsibility for child care is dispersed throughout several government departments with little co-ordination between departments.

The system has created a population of children who have been "left out on their own" on the margins of society. The recommendations, outlined in this report, emerged from the collective experiences and concerns of those directly involved in service delivery for young people leaving care. If these children are to be brought back into society, the government must take these recommendations seriously and implement them as a matter of urgency.

1.5 STRUCTURE OF STUDY

Following this executive summary, the study is presented in a further five chapters.

Chapter 2 introduces the study by summarising the evolution of the Irish child care system and by outlining the methodologies used in the study.

Chapter 3 examines young people who are discharged from special schools. It looks at reasons why young people were placed in special schools, their family background characteristics, their circumstances and destination on leaving care. It tracks these young people six months after leaving care and again two years after leaving care.

Chapter 4 examines the circumstances of young people leaving health board care. It contrasts the circumstances of health board care leavers with young people who are discharged from special schools.

Chapter 5 focuses on young people in the Eastern Health Board region who encounter difficulties getting a care placement.

Chapter 6 focuses on young people who leave probation hostels funded by the Probation and Welfare Service.

2

Background

This is a study about young people who are leaving the care of the state. It includes young people leaving the care of health boards and young people who are being released from special schools which are the responsibility of the Department of Education and Science and probation hostels which are the responsibility of the Department of Justice, Equality and Law Reform. Its specific focus is on the young people themselves and on their destination on leaving care.

The transition to adulthood for most young people is difficult as they are challenged to make decisions regarding major aspects of their life, for example, education, career and living arrangements. Most young people have family and networks of social support to call upon at times of challenge and of major decisions in their lives. In contrast, young care leavers are often alone, isolated and severed from family and support networks. Moreover, they are often expected to make the transition to adulthood abruptly and at a young age.

There are a number of studies on young people in health board care and on young juvenile offenders. These suggest that these young people are predominantly from a lower-income background and more likely to experience poverty, unemployment and accommodation difficulties than young people with a non-care background (Flynn, 1967; Hart, 1968, 1969; Burke *et al.*, 1981; O'Mahony, 1985; Richardson, 1985; O'Gorman and Barnes, 1991; Fahy-Bates, 1996; O'Higgins, 1996; Clarke, 1998). Notwithstanding this, Stein (1997) maintains that the disadvantage experienced by care leavers later in life, in terms of education achievement, unemployment and dependency on welfare, cannot be explained by social class origins alone. The experience of care has an independent effect on the disadvantage experienced later in life. Factors identified in the literature include the emotional stress of being taken into care, low expectations of carers and teachers, abuse while in care, and the disruption caused by placement moves. In addition, the stigma attached to being in care, and the fact that many young people in care are given insufficient knowledge about their family backgrounds and thus have difficulty making sense of their past, have all been found to contribute to the disadvantaged position of care leavers.

Research on leaving care also points to the need for preparation for leaving care to begin at the point of admission and not just prior to the point of exit. The concept of leaving care is thus sometimes referred to as "through-care". In Ireland, as far back as 1970, the Kennedy Report[1] emphasised the need to view dischargement and aftercare as an integral part of the child care system. It is in this context that the in-care system and juvenile justice system has relevance to the present study.

Staff in Focus Ireland had observed that many young people who became homeless and accessed Focus Ireland's services had a care background. Hence, Focus Ireland commissioned the present study to raise awareness of the difficulties faced by many care leavers. If the needs of the young people could be met while in care or on leaving care, homelessness in some cases could be prevented. Although there are several Irish studies on the characteristics of young people in care and on young juvenile offenders, there are no large-scale studies on what happens to young people after they leave care and to young offenders after their release. This report aims to fill this vacuum.

The present study builds on the methodologies developed by the Leeds University Leaving Care Research Project (LLCRP) which was published in 1992 (Biehal, Clayden, Stein and Wade), and the leaving care study carried out in Northern Ireland by Pinkerton and McCrea (1996). It outlines the circum-

---

[1] Reformatory and Industrial Schools Systems Report, 1970.

stances of 165 young people leaving health board care and institutions for young people who are in trouble with the law
(special school and probation hostel). The circumstances of
young people six months after leaving care and again two years
after leaving care are also examined.

2.1 EVOLUTION OF THE CARE SYSTEM

Children in the care of the state have elicited considerable attention from professionals and the public over the last decade.
In the 1990s several high-profile court cases and public inquiries into child abuse focused public attention on children in
care. This revival of interest in children in care is in stark contrast to the previous 100 years where the lack of interest is reflected in the minimum changes enacted in child care policy
and legislation. It took almost 100 years to change the *Children
Act, 1908* which remained the main legislative basis for child
care, with only few additional reforms, until the full enactment
of the *Child Care Act, 1991* in mid-1996.[2]

The 19th Century

Robins (1980) in *The Lost Children* traces the historical evolution
of the modern child care system to its origins in the industrial
and reformatory school system of the 19th century. The term
"destitute children" was used interchangeably with children
who were "orphaned", "abandoned", "impoverished", "de-
praved", and more recently "deprived", "disturbed" and "difficult". These are children who are removed from the custody
of their parents, either voluntarily or compulsorily, when parents are considered to have failed in their parental duty. These
children then become the responsibility of the state, or what
Robins terms "children of the state".

State provision of residential child care in Ireland started in
1838 when the workhouse was the main provision for children
who needed care. As the 19th century progressed, there was a
growing awareness of the inappropriateness of the workhouse

---

[2] The legislation governing the provision for young people in care and leaving care is outlined in Appendix 2.

for children. Many children were also being incarcerated in adult prisons. Private charity organisations and religious-controlled institutions intervened to make a response. The *Reformatory Schools (Youthful Offenders) Act, 1858* was introduced. This Act certified a number of existing voluntary institutions and homes as suitable for the reception of young offenders committed through the courts. It also provided for the inspection of these institutions (Kennedy, 1970). The first reformatory school, St. Kevin's Reformatory School in Glencree, County Wicklow, was opened in 1859. By 1870 there were ten reformatory schools, five for girls and five for boys. The function of reformatory schools was to provide reformative treatment for young offenders between the ages of 12 and 16 years.

The need for a different type of institution was recognised and nine years later, in 1868 St. Joseph's Industrial School for Girls, High Park, Dublin was opened by the Sisters of Our Lady of Charity of Refuge. A year later, St. Mary's Industrial School for Girls at Lakelands, Dublin was opened by the Irish Sisters of Charity. The number of schools reached its maximum in 1898 when there were 71 schools with almost 8,000 young people resident in them. The industrial schools had to be approved by the state and subjected to an annual inspection.

The placement of children under five years of age in foster care (known as boarding out) was provided for in the *Poor Law Amendment Act, 1862* and the *Infant Life Protection Act, 1897.*[3]

CHILDREN ACT, 1908

The *Children Act, 1908* consolidated 19th-century legislation. It dealt with children in need of care and protection as well as providing for juvenile offenders. Children were taken into care under Section 24 of the Act, which provided for a Place of Safety Order if the child was considered by the district court to be at immediate risk. Alternatively, a Fit Person Order on the child could be secured if the district court had reason to believe that

---

[3] The system of fostering was later amended by the *Health Act 1953* and the *Boarding Out Regulations of 1954 and 1983*, until they were superseded by the *Child Care Act, 1991*.

the young person was being neglected or was out of control or convicted of his or her first offence. A Fit Person Order gives the person named in the order "Like control of the child or young person as if he were his parent". A Fit Person includes any society or corporate body established for the reception or protection of children. Under the Act, children could also be placed in care voluntarily.[4]

Under the Act, the age of criminal responsibility is 7 years and a young offender is a person between the ages of 7 and 16 years who has been found guilty by the courts of committing a crime. The Act provides for the setting up of special children's courts. Whereas reformatory schools aimed primarily to provide service for offenders, industrial schools, on the other hand, aimed to provide care for children who had not committed an offence. Industrial schools catered for various categories of deprived children such as those found begging, as well as orphaned or destitute children. Under the Act, children whose parents were unable to control them, children who gave trouble in workhouses, first-time offenders, offenders between the ages of 7 and 12 and persistent truants could be committed to industrial schools.[5] Underlying factors relating to the placement of children in industrial schools included poverty, illegitimacy, abandonment and the committal of minor offences. The role of the industrial schools was inextricably linked to that of reformatory schools, as industrial schools also accepted young offenders where the offence committed was a first offence and not serious and where it was considered that the child would not exercise an evil influence over other children.

Mid-20th Century Developments

Responsibility for industrial schools and reformatory schools was transferred from the Minister for Justice to the Minister for

---

[4] From 1953 until it was superseded by the enactment of the *Child Care Act, 1991*, the *Health Act, 1953* governed the admission of children who were taken into care voluntarily.

[5] Truancy was later governed by the *School Attendance Act, 1926* (and as amended in 1936 and 1967). Children prosecuted could be sent to an industrial school.

Education in 1924. Until the 1970s when the health boards were
established, the system of child care was under one Minister,
namely the Minister for Education. The reformatory and industrial school buildings were large, old-style institutions, many of
which were geographically isolated and poorly financed.[6] The
largest of the institutions, in Artane, Dublin, catered for 800
boys.

The system that developed in the mid-19th century was not
appreciably altered until the 1970s. These institutions were
what Goffman (1971) referred to as "total institutions". All aspects of life including education, recreation, eating and sleeping for large numbers of people were conducted in the same
place and under one authority. Institutional provision for large
numbers of people inevitably leads to authoritarian regimes in
which surveillance of inmates to ensure compliance is an important element of the system. Many of the young people when
they left continued an institutional way of life, living-in in hospitals, entering the armed forces or the navy or taking up domestic service work in large institutions (Kennedy, 1970). It is
not surprising that many people with an institutionalised care
background ended up later in life institutionalised in hostels for
the single homeless (McCarthy, 1988).

Although many of the institutions were closed prior to the
publication of the Kennedy Report in 1970, the report is seen as
a turning point in child care history (Ferguson and Kenny,
1995). Although the Kennedy Report did not draw attention to
the physical or sexual abuse which was later found to be taking
place in many of these institutions, it documented the need to
de-institutionalise the care system in line with modern thinking.
Proponents of de-institutionalisation emphasised fostering and
proclaimed that fostering should be the preferred form of care.
Where residential care was necessary, smaller units should be
developed.

When the Kennedy Report was published, the number of
children in care was approximately 5,000.[7] These included
young people in reformatory schools, industrial schools, re-

---

[6] See J. Robins, *The Lost Children*, Institute of Public Administration, 1980.

[7] This figure is estimated from data provided in the Kennedy Report.

mand homes, other approved institutions, non-approved voluntary homes and young people who were "boarded out" by the local health authorities. Just over one-quarter of the care population was boarded out. The estimate of 5,000 did not include children in County Homes, Magedlan Homes or young people placed in employment by local authorities. The actual figure of children in care was approximately 8,000.

Alongside the emphasis on de-institutionalisation, the Kennedy Report focused on the need for a child-centred system, which would take into consideration the emotional and psychological needs of the child. It recommended that staff employed should be professionally trained and that assessment centres be introduced to assess the needs of the young people coming into the system. It also identified the need to raise the age of criminal responsibility to 12 years and to put in place an effective aftercare service for young people leaving care.

Today there are approximately 3,600 children in health board care, 162 young people in special schools run by the Department of Education and Science, 32 of whom are on remand and 45 young people in Probation and Welfare Service hostels. In contrast to the 1970s, foster care is now firmly established as the most important source of alternative family care for children in health board care. In 1970, only one-quarter of children and young people in health board care were in foster care, then known as boarded out. In 1996, 76 per cent of children in health board care were in foster care. It is interesting to note that approximately 12 per cent of the children in foster care are in care with relatives.

2.2 FRAGMENTED POLICY FRAMEWORK

A key recommendation of the Kennedy Report (1970) and later the Task Force Report (1980)[8] was that legislation relating to child care be incorporated into a composite child care act.

---

[8] The Task Force on Child Care Services was established in 1973 to make recommendations on the extension of services for deprived children and children at risk, to prepare a Bill updating the law in relation to children and to make recommendations on whatever administrative reforms it considered necessary in the child care services.

These reports also recommended that responsibility for child care be unified in one government department, namely the Department of Health. The responsibility of the Department would include school attendance services, detention services for young offenders, probation services for young people and service for young people at risk. This did not happen. The early 1990s presented an opportunity to undertake a radical restructuring of the child care system. What emerged was a dual system of care with separate pieces of legislation governing the health board system and the special schools for young offenders run by the Department of Education. The introduction of legislation, i.e. the *Child Care Act, 1991,* for young people whose welfare is at risk and the proposed introduction of legislation for young offenders[9] copperfastened a dual system of child care. The weaknesses which emerged as a result of this dual system of child care are referred to throughout the present report.

There are now two separate care systems for young people at risk. One is the responsibility of the Department of Health and Children and the second is the responsibility of the Department of Education and Science. The Department of Health was given a central role in the child care system in 1974 and many of the industrial schools were brought under its authority. In 1984, it was given full responsibility for young people who are at risk or in need of care and protection. The health boards cater for young people up until the age of 18 years. The majority of children in health board care are now placed in foster care[10] and in smaller residential units known as adolescent units or group homes. These services are now governed by the *Child Care Act, 1991* and its related regulations.

The majority of juveniles who commit a crime are dealt with through a process of informal and formal cautioning by the gardai under the Juvenile Diversion Programme introduced in

---

[9] The *Children Bill, 1999* is to replace the *Children Act, 1908* and other enactments relating to juvenile justice.

[10] In 1996, 76 per cent of children and young people in care were in foster care.

1963.[11] The Department of Education and Science is responsible for the five special schools, which cater primarily, though not exclusively, for young people who have been committed by the courts. Despite promises by successive governments to introduce juvenile justice legislation to repeal the remaining provisions of the *Children Act, 1908*, legislation has not yet been introduced. Currently, it is proposed to introduce the *Children Bill, 1999*, which will raise the age of criminal responsibility from 7 to 12 years of age. It also brings the legislation for juvenile offenders into line with the welfare principles advocated in the *United Nations Convention on the Rights of the Child* where the best interests of the child are given primary consideration. The Juvenile Liaison/Diversion programme is to be put on a statutory basis under the Bill and provision for convening family welfare conferences are provided for.

Child care legislation is outlined in Appendix 1 of the study.

Increasing Awareness of the Needs of Children

Several high-profile court cases and public inquiries over the last decade have focused public attention on child abuse and in particular on child sexual abuse in families and in residential care settings in Ireland. Investigations into child abuse within families included *The Kilkenny Incest Investigation*, which involved a 27-year-old woman who from the age of 10 had endured extreme physical and sexual abuse from her father. During this time, the victim had been hospitalised several times, had numerous contacts with the out-patient casualty department and it is estimated by Buckley *et al.* (1997) that she had over 100 contacts with social service agencies in the South-Eastern Health Board Region.[12] The deliberations of the investi-

---

[11] The Juvenile Diversion Programme run by the Garda Juvenile Liaison Officer (JLO) scheme is an alternative to bringing the young person before the court who if found guilty could result in a criminal record. The programme provides for the cautioning of juvenile offenders who are less than 18 years.

[12] From the age of 10 years to 16 years, she had attended the GP nine times with abuse-related injuries which included abrasions, swellings, sprains and scalds. During this time she was also referred to the x-ray departments where she was x-rayed for injuries to her knee, her finger and a strain in her arm. Between the ages of 16 and 18 years she attended pre-natal and ante-natal

gation were published in 1993 (McGuinness, 1993). The publication was to have a profound influence on speeding up the enactment of the *Child Care Act, 1991*.

In 1995, Joseph McColgan, a west of Ireland farmer, was convicted of raping and abusing his children over a 20-year period. He was sentenced to 12 years in prison. In July 1998, a review group established by the North-Western Health Board published a report on the case, *West of Ireland Farmer Case*. This detailed the systematic emotional and sexual abuse of the four children by their father. Despite numerous contacts with the accident and emergency departments of hospitals, general practitioners, social workers, public health nurses and gardai, the system failed to protect the children from the horrendous abuse being inflicted on them. The story of one of the survivors of this abuse is documented by McKay (1998) in *Sophia's Story*.

In 1996, an investigation was undertaken into the death of Kelly Fitzgerald in the Western Health Board and the report *Kelly: A Child is Dead* was published in 1996.

Abuse in residential care has been unfolding since the beginning of the 1990s and there is now substantial evidence that many children in industrial and reformatory schools were brutally abused. Several cases have been processed through the courts. Two television series, *Dear Daughter* and *States of Fear*, highlighted the fact that abuse took place in residential care. The book *Suffer the Little Children* (Rafferty and O'Sullivan, 1999) was based on *States of Fear*.

---

services. She revealed to the services that her father was the father of her child. When she was 20 years (1985) she told the social services of the persistent sexual assault. She told the GP of the violence. The GP told the gardai and the gardai told the social services. Nothing was done. During the time she was 20 to 27 years, she attended Casualty/Outpatient Departments at least 10 times and was admitted at least three times. A litany of injuries were identified which included bruising on the upper arms, back, lacerations to head and fracture on middle finger, abdominal pains and pains in the kidneys. Finally, in January 1992 when she was hospitalised for an injury to her eye which nearly left her blind, the gardai were notified on the advice of the GP. The hospital also informed the social work services. In March 1993, at the Central Criminal Court, her father, then 48 years of age, was given a 7 year sentence having pleaded guilty to a total of 56 charges which included rape, incest and assault.

The public is thus becoming increasingly aware that child abuse is taking place both at home in families and in residential care settings. Many of the children who were abandoned, neglected or abused at home in families have been reabused in residential settings. Gogarty (1996) states that children need to be helped to come to terms with this "double trauma of abuse" and to repair the loss, trauma and emotional consequences of such abuse.

As a result of the high-profile cases, the enactment of the *Child Care Act, 1991* was speeded up. The Irish government signed the *United Nations Convention on the Rights of the Child* in 1992, which had been adopted by the United Nations General Assembly in November 1989. This Convention emphasises the importance of empowering young people and affirms their right to participate in decisions that affect their lives. Article 19 of the Convention states that parties shall take all appropriate legislative, administrative, social and educational measures to protect the child from all forms of physical or mental violence, injury or abuse while in the care of parent(s), legal guardian(s), or any other person who has care of the child. The Convention also obliges governments to present periodic reports to the UN Committee on the Rights of the Child and to outline the extent to which the rights as guaranteed in the Convention are being adhered to.

As a direct result of the *Kilkenny Incest Investigation*, the government in 1995 introduced the guidelines *Notification of Suspected Cases of Child Abuse between Health Boards and Gardai.* These guidelines aimed to improve the co-ordination between the health boards and the gardai. These were introduced to complement the *Child Abuse Guidelines*[13] introduced in 1987. Finally in 1999, new national guidelines, *Children First: National Guidelines for the Protection and Welfare of Children,* were published to assist in the identification, reporting, and management of child abuse.

---

[13] *Guidelines on Procedures for the Identification, Investigation and Management of Child Abuse.*

In 1995, *Child Care Regulations* were introduced in regard to the placement of children in residential care, foster care and the placement of children with relatives.

In 1996, the Department of Health and Children introduced a set of further regulations pertaining to residential care, *The Child Care (Standards in Children's Residential Centres) Regulations, 1996,* and a *Guide to Good Practice in Children's Residential Centres.*

The standards relate to the following:

- Care practice and operation policy

- Staffing

- Accommodation

- Access arrangements

- Fire precautions

- Record keeping.

The *Guide to Good Practice* advises that each unit should have a written statement defining the purpose of the centre, including the population it caters for, and the service it aims to provide. The *Guide* also outlines the principles underlying good practice.

In 1998, under Part VIII of the *Child Care Act, 1991* a Registration and Inspection Service was established for residential homes which are operated by voluntary bodies, the purpose of which is to ensure compliance with legislation and provide standards of good practice.

The Ombudsman for Children, which was first announced by the government in 1996, has not yet been designated. An ombudsman is important in that it will provide parents and young people with an independent mechanism of appeal to have their rights to services enforced.

As a result of public outrage and anger generated by the television series *States of Fear*, the Taoiseach gave an apology to the victims of childhood abuse and set up a Commission to Inquire into Childhood Abuse to hear publicly the testimony of survivors of abuse. The government also made £4 million available for counselling for adult survivors of institutional and other forms of abuse. The shame and humiliation surrounding abuse and neglect, which bound survivors of abuse to silence, has been lifted. Church, state and society are now obliged to listen to their stories.

In November 1999, the government established an interdepartmental group to oversee the preparation of a national children's strategy. The strategy will outline the policy direction for child care practice for the next ten years.

Lack of Residential Places

Despite the many changes taking place in child care policy and provision, the operation of the residential child care system still faces major difficulties. Although foster care is the main form of care, residential care is required for young people for whom foster care is not suitable. The lack of residential places for young people with specialised needs has been highlighted throughout the 1990s.

Part of the problem results from the inflexible nature of the present system and the reluctance of the three main government departments with responsibility for children and young people, namely the Departments of Education and Science, Health and Children and Justice, Equality and Law Reform, to assume responsibility for young people with specialised needs. This has led one high court judge to blame the "administrative torpor and absence of planning" for the lack of adequate facilities.[14]

The high court has become a place of last resort and a battleground for young people who are attempting to enforce their rights to accommodation and services. A landmark precedent was established in 1995, when a minor sued the Ministers for Education and Health and the Attorney General on the basis that his constitutional rights to be accommodated and educated had not been fulfilled. The court ruled that where a child has special needs which cannot be met by the parents or guardian, the state has an obligation to cater for their needs. As a result of

---

[14] See "Judge Blames 'Administrative Torpor' for Lack of Places for Problem Children", *Irish Times,* 5 December 1998.

this and subsequent cases, health boards are obliged to provide secure places, where necessary, for children who require them (Durcan, 1997).

Numerous young people took their cases to court in the second half of the 1990s as young troubled teenagers who have not committed a crime were being sent to remand centres. These included a young teenage boy with a mental handicap who was homeless for a year and a young boy who was autistic who had not committed an offence. More recently, in the absence of suitable alternatives, young vulnerable boys who have not committed a crime have been sent to a juvenile prison[15] or adult psychiatric hospitals.[16]

The placement of young people who have not committed a crime in remand centres has resulted in places not being available for juveniles who have committed a crime. At one particular time, half of the remand places at Oberstown Girls Centre were taken up by girls who had not committed an offence, but were placed there under high court orders because of the lack of suitable health board accommodation.[17] They were essentially homeless and were placed in the centre by the high court because their "moral and physical welfare was considered to be at risk if they remained on the streets". This practice of detaining young people who have not committed a crime in a remand/assessment centre and juvenile prisons is contrary to the *Child Care Act, 1991* and the ethos of the *United Nations Convention on the Rights of the Child* which was signed by the Irish government in 1992.

In 1999, 22 young people who needed specialised care which was not available, were placed in residential care outside the state. Also, in the absence of sufficient secure places,

---

[15] "State and EHB Admit They have no Suitable Place to Send Troubled and Vulnerable Boy", *Irish Times,* 24 March 1999.

[16] "Judge Berates State on Care of Children", *Irish Times*, 17 March 2000.

[17] "Remand Shortage Leads to Dropped Charges", *Irish Times*, 18 October 1997.

staff of security firms are caring for 17 young people in the Eastern Health Board region.[18]

The government has announced plans to develop an additional 110 high-support and special care places nationally. The Minister of State with special responsibility for child care has recently announced that a new interim body on special residential services for children convicted of committing offences and children who have behavioural problems and are in need of special care and protection is being set up. The new interim body will advise the Ministers for Health and Children and Education and Science on policy on the remand and detention of children in detention schools and special care units. The Residential Services Board provided for under the *Children Bill, 1999* will replace the interim board when the bill is enacted.

Care Staff

It is a difficult and challenging time for care workers and many residential centres are finding it difficult to recruit care workers. Morale is low among staff as a result of the high level of publicity surrounding abuse in residential care settings (McCarthy, 1996). A recent study, *Lives in Care* (Clarke, 1998), surveys 16 residential centres run by the Religions Sisters of Mercy (RSM). Care staff face uncertainly in regard to the appropriate level of contact that they should have with children and young people. They fear that any type of physical contact may be mistaken and lead to an allegation of abuse. Strict regulations are now in place in most residential homes to safeguard both children and workers. The report sees the need for a code of appropriate contact between staff and children, which allows both parties to feel comfortable.[19]

The Irish Care Workers Association has pointed to the need for strategies for dealing with allegations of abuse. They assert that the principles of natural justice should prevail when allegations of abuse are made and that care workers should be

[18] "TD Critical of Arrangements for Children Needing Special Care", *Irish Times,* 1 January 2000.
[19] "Home Went Too Far Banning Physical Contact", *Irish Times*, 16 October 1998.

considered innocent until they are proven guilty. The Association also points to the need for a proper registration and licensing system for care workers.

2.3 RESEARCH POPULATION

The research population comprised three sub-groupings:

- Young people leaving the care of the country's five special schools for young offenders

- Young people leaving the care of three health board regions (the Eastern, North-Eastern and North-Western Health Board regions), which were selected in order to get an overview of the circumstances of young people from a range of geographical backgrounds

- Young people leaving the care of the two Dublin probation hostels.

Leaving care studies have tended to focus on young people who are 15 years or over. However, key informants pointed out that many young people in Ireland are leaving care as young as 13, because of the breakdown of care placements. For this reason, it was decided to include in the current study young people leaving care who are 13 years or older.

Initially it was decided to identify the leaving care population over a six-month time period between April and September 1997. Staff in special schools, however, pointed out that there were likely to be very low numbers of young people leaving special schools during a time period of six months. They proposed an 18-month period, which would generate a larger study population, and so an 18-month time period was decided on for the special schools, with a six-month time period for the three health boards and the two probation hostels.

The research population was thus defined as follows:

- Young people of 13 years or over who had spent a minimum of two months in a special school and had left the school or were placed "out on licence" under the supervision of the

Probation and Welfare Service between April 1996 and September 1997

* Young people of 13 years or over who had spent a minimum of two months in the care of one of the three health boards included in the study and had left the care of and ceased to be supported by the health board between April 1997 and September 1997

* Young people who left either of the two Dublin probation hostels between April 1997 and September 1997.

2.4 LEAVING CARE LEGISLATION

Under the *Child Care Act, 1991* young people can remain in the care of a health board until they are 18 years of age. Section 45 of the 1991 Act empowers a health board to provide "aftercare" support for children in their care. Assistance *may* be given in the following ways: visiting the young person at home, arranging for the completion of his or her education and arranging for hostel or other forms of accommodation by co-operating with housing authorities in planning accommodation. Assistance can be offered until the young person reaches the age of 21. This represents a significant extension of health board powers in relation to aftercare and enables health boards to take responsibility for the welfare of young people once they leave care. The Act and the accompanying Regulations make it clear that preparation for leaving care should begin well before a young person ceases to be looked after and that preparation should commence two years prior to leaving care.

This legislation which is enabling rather than obligatory, significantly weakens the legislative basis of leaving care practice. In addition, the fact that the Department of Health and Children has not issued a written policy or established procedures to assist young people leaving care means that initiatives are at the discretion of individual health boards.

Special schools, which are the responsibility of the Minister for Education and Science, are still governed by the *Children Act, 1908.* For the most part young people leave special schools at 16 years of age. Only minimal provision is made for aftercare, which allows provision for the young person to be placed under the supervision of a probation and welfare officer on release from a children's detention centre. The *Children Bill 1999,* which is to supersede the remaining provision of the 1908 Act, does not strengthen the basis on which aftercare is provided and there is no legislative basis for special schools themselves to provide aftercare.

Unlike England and Northern Ireland, care leavers in the Republic of Ireland do not have specific rights to aftercare support. In England, the *Children Act 1989* and in Northern Ireland the *Children (NI) Order of 1993* place a duty on local authorities to advise and befriend young people under 21 years. They also have a duty to accommodate any child in need who has reached the age of 16 and whose welfare, otherwise, is likely to be seriously prejudiced. They are empowered to liaise with other public agencies, including education, housing and health authorities to enable them to comply with their duties and to provide accommodation and other appropriate services. Furthermore, every local authority has to establish procedures for considering any representation or complaint from young people with regard to their preparation for leaving care or aftercare services (Pinkerton and Stein, 1995). In addition, the needs of children with special needs (mental illness or physical or mental disability) and young people with diverse ethnic identities are recognised in the legislation in Northern Ireland and England.

2.5 IDENTIFICATION OF AND TRACKING OF RESEARCH POPULATION

Focus Ireland met with personnel from the Department of Health and Children and the Department of Education and Science to explain the purpose of the research and to elicit their support for the research. Meetings were also held with senior personnel of the three health boards. A further meeting was held with the senior social workers of the three health boards to discuss the procedure for collecting data. It was decided that the social work managers would identify the numbers and names of young people leaving care in each Community Care

Area. They would request the social worker dealing with each young person to fill out a monitoring form when the young person was leaving care, and again six months and two years after he or she had left care. The research team offered to help individual social workers with filling out monitoring forms if requested.

This procedure for identifying the leaving care population presented problems in the Eastern Health Board region. All except one social work manager were unable to identify the numbers leaving care in their areas. They did, however, offer to put the researchers in touch with the team leaders and social workers to identify the leaving care population, but attempts to arrange meetings with these staff members proved cumbersome. Time was running out and a lot of the resources of the project were being devoted to identifying the research population.

It was then decided to request the administrative section of the Eastern Health Board to identify all young people leaving the care of the Eastern Health Board during the period April to September 1997. It was proposed that the names then be forwarded to the relevant senior social work managers, who would be requested to return the monitoring forms to Focus Ireland by a specified date. However, the administrative section was also unable to provide a list of young people leaving care in the six-month period of the study. The final listing was compiled by staff in Focus Ireland, who made contact by telephone with all residential units in the Eastern Health Board area to ascertain the numbers of young people leaving their care during the time period of the study. This list was combined with the names of young people identified by social work managers, team leaders and individual social workers with whom the researchers made contact.

Although there was also a delay in collecting information from the two other health board regions, this did not appear to be as a result of the difficulties in identifying the leaving care population.

Data collection from special schools for young offenders and the Probation and Welfare Service was not problematic. Four of the five schools filled out monitoring forms and returned them to the researchers. In the case of one special school, the researcher filled out the monitoring forms, together with relevant staff.

Tracking Procedure for Health Board Population

The main procedure for tracking the young people involved social workers filling out forms on the circumstances of young people at three different intervals: on leaving care, six months after leaving care and two years after leaving care. Where the individual social worker did not wish to provide the researchers with the name of the young person, the initials of the young person and the date of birth was used as an identifier. It was agreed that the social workers would keep a special file on any information that would be useful in tracking the young person six months or two years after the young person had left care. If the social worker had left his or her post they would inform an appropriate person, such as the team leader or the social work manager, and hand over the file which was to be available for the purpose of the leaving care study.

The changeover of social workers created difficulties for the tracking process in two of the health board regions, i.e. the Eastern Health Board and the North-Eastern Health Board. It did not create a difficulty in the North-Western Health Board Region as the same people, i.e. the team leader and four social workers, were available to fill out the forms on all three occasions.

In the Eastern Health Board Region, 31 social workers filled out the initial form and the form for young people six months after they had left care. By the end of the two-year interval, 14 (45 per cent) of the 31 social workers were not in their original positions. The 14 social workers had responsibility for 16 young people. Three (30 per cent) of the ten social workers in the North-Eastern Health Board Region had changed during the two- year period. This involved four young people.

The changeover of social workers combined with the fact that in some cases the researchers only had the initials of the young care leaver, created inordinate difficulties for the research. This was further compounded by the fact that in some instances team leaders and social work managers had also changed.

Although individual social workers were co-operative, ease of access to the social work service itself varied a great deal. In many cases getting an answer to a telephone call was extremely difficult. In some cases the phone at reception was left to ring out. In other cases it was continually engaged. In some cases, when the phone was answered and the social workers were not available, there was no facility to leave a message. The use of mobile phones or a personal answering service by social workers in these instances would have been useful.

For four young people, over 40 telephone calls were made in each case to track the file of the young person.

Where the social worker was unsure of the circumstances of the young person or had not had recent contact with the young person or did not feel that they could make contact, a combination of sources was used to supplement and cross-check information. This included support workers in Focus Housing, contacts in community organisations, particularly in the areas of Ballymun, North Inner City and Clondalkin, and contacts with individual officers from the Probation and Welfare Service (P&WS). A search was also undertaken on prison records to determine if and when any of the young people from the leaving care population were in prison. We were informed that it would not be possible to undertake a search of the social welfare database.

Tracking Procedure for Special Schools

Getting the three sets of forms filled out by staff in the special schools did not prove a major difficulty. Forms were filled out by key workers, or unit managers. Where the special school had no contact with the young person, information was obtained from officers from the local Probation and Welfare Service, direct contact with families, the young people themselves and through informal contact with the friends of the young person. One school employed a staff member for over a two-week period to track the young people.

Interviewing Young People

Thirty young people were interviewed for the study. We felt that it was important to interview young people in order to get their views and to give them a voice. It was hoped that all young people interviewed would form part of the study population. However, it was only possible to make contact with 13 young people who were part of the study population. The 13 young people comprised six young people who had been in special schools, two young people who had been in foster care, three young people who had been in health board residential care, two of whom had ended up homeless and attended the out-of-hours service.

Reasons why we were unable to interview more young people from the study population included the fact the social workers had lost contact with the young person. In some cases where social workers had contact with the young person they felt that they could not ask the young person if they wished to be interviewed. In addition, some young people had left Ireland and were not available for interview. In the absence of being able to get the quota from the study population for interview, an additional 17 young people who had been in care but are not in the study population were interviewed.

The 30 young people who were interviewed included: Ten young people from special schools, ten young people from residential care, six young people from foster care and four young people who were homeless.

3

Young People Leaving Special Schools

"You can't ring home. The only way to have contact is to write. I can't write. My mother has ten kids and my father is sick. They are not able to come to visit me. It's lonely. You get locked up in the cell at 7.15 for the night. It is a tiny cell." — Young care leaver who ended up in prison

Over the two-year research period, three forms were filled out on each of the young people leaving the care of special schools. The first form concerned the characteristics and circumstances of the young people on leaving care, the second form concerned their situation six months after leaving care and the third form concerned their situation two years after leaving care.

Six months after leaving the care of special school, 90 per cent (93) of the original 103 population of young people were tracked and two years after leaving care 88 per cent (91) were tracked.

Staff in special schools filled out the first form from confidential case files. Where special schools had no contact with the young person, information on the situation of the young person six months after leaving care and two years after leaving care was gained from a variety of sources. These included direct contact with the young person or the family of the young person, informal contact with friends of the young person and contact with officers from the local Probation and Welfare Service.

With the co-operation of residential care workers, the researchers constructed case histories on over 50 young people. Personal interviews were also held with ten young people who had left special schools.

The researchers wish to acknowledge the time and energy given by staff to tracing young people after they had left care, which in some cases was particularly difficult.

3.1 SPECIAL SCHOOLS FOR YOUNG OFFENDERS

The Special Schools

There are five[1] special schools for young offenders funded by the Department of Education and Science. Between them, they provide approximately 130 residential places (see Table 3.1).

St. Joseph's and the National Care and Education Unit, formally known as St. Laurence's, are certified industrial schools and cater for boys in the younger age groups.[2] St. Joseph's, in Clonmel, which opened in 1883, is run by the Rosminian Order. The original buildings were replaced and a new modern open centre was opened in 1990. St Laurence's was purpose-built in 1972.

Oberstown Boys' Centre and Trinity House are certified reformatory schools where young males who have been convicted of an imprisonable offence are committed by the courts. They were established to replace the reformatory of St. Conleth's School, Daingean, Co. Offaly that was run by the Oblate fathers and was closed in the late 1960s. Established in 1972, Oberstown was originally administered by the Oblate Fathers until they withdrew from the service and the state failed to maintain it. The school was closed in the early 1980s and re-opened in 1993. It is a semi-secure unit and it shares a campus with Trinity House, which was opened in 1983. Trinity House is the only secure unit for young males under 16 years in Ireland.

---

[1] This listing does not include centres for remand and assessment. The National Assessment and Remand Unit, formerly known as St. Michael's Remand and Assessment, in Finglas has twenty places. Oberstown Boys' Centre provides ten remand places. Boys from seven to sixteen years can be remanded for periods varying from one day to several months while awaiting a court decision. Trinity House provides two places for boys on remand. Oberstown Girls Centre provides seven remand and assessment places for girls.

[2] Due to the fact that the National Care and Education Unit was known as St. Laurence's when the study commenced, the name St. Laurence's is retained.

Table 3.1: Special Schools

Unit	Legal Status	Number Catered For	Gender Catered For	Age on Admission	Referral Procedure	Normal Length of Stay
St Joseph's, Clonmel	Industrial school	40	Male	9–13	Referred by courts/health board	Long-term (up to 4 years)
St Laurence's, Finglas	Industrial school	35	Male	10–15	Referred by courts/health board	1–2 years
Oberstown Boys' Centre, Lusk	Reformatory school	20	Male	12–16	Referred by courts	Long-term (up to 4 years)
Trinity House, Lusk	Reformatory school	28	Male	12–16	Referred by courts	2–4 years
Oberstown Girls' Centre, Lusk	Reformatory school	8	Female	12–16	Referred by courts	Long-term

Oberstown Girls' Centre is the only special school for girls. It is a certified reformatory school where young girls are placed by the courts for an imprisonable offence.[3]

With the exception of St Joseph's, the special schools are managed by boards of management appointed by the Department of Education and Science. There is also a probation and welfare officer assigned to each special school.

Leaving-care Population of the Special Schools

Tables 3.2 and 3.3 show the numbers and gender of young people in the study population.

Table 3.2: Study Population

Unit	Number	Percentage
Trinity House	27	26.2
St. Joseph's	31	30.0
Oberstown Boys' Centre	21	20.4
St. Laurence's	19	18.5
Oberstown Girls' Centre	5	4.9
Total	103	100.0

Given that four of the five special schools cater for boys, it is not surprising that the majority of the leaving-care population are male.

Table 3.3: Study Population by Gender

Gender	Number	Percentage
Male	98	95.1
Female	5	4.9
Total	103	100

---

[3] While Oberstown Girls Centre has provided accommodation for young girls in the care of the health board, this is not its official function.

Young people with a Traveller background made up just under 12 per cent (12) of the population.

None of the young people leaving the care of the special school had children.

Family Circumstances

There is a high incidence of disruption in the lives of the young people who enter special schools. Almost all come from lower-income backgrounds. Poverty tended to be combined with other personal and inter-personal difficulties within the family. These ranged from relationship breakdown, addiction, family conflict and family violence. The following table indicates that only 37 per cent of the parents of young people in the study are living together, 15 per cent are widowed and 45 per cent are living apart.

Table 3.4: Marital Status of Parents

Marital status	Number	Percentage
Married and/or living together	38	36.9
Married but living apart	38	36.9
Unmarried and living apart	8	7.7
Widowed	15	14.6
Other	4	3.9
Total	103	100.0

Only 6 per cent of mothers and 23 per cent of fathers are in full-time employment, indicating that the majority of families are dependent on social welfare.

The great majority of families (78 per cent) live in local authority housing. A further 9 per cent either live in trailers or tents or are of no fixed abode and 4 per cent live in the private rented sector. Only 10 per cent own their own houses. Over a third (35 per cent) of young people in the study had siblings who have been in care.

The vast majority (98 per cent) of young people in care have siblings, and 80 per cent have three or more siblings.

Table 3.5: Number of Siblings of Young People in Study

Number of Siblings	No. of Young People in Study Having this No. of Siblings	Percentage of Young People in Study
None	2	1.9
1–2	18	17.6
3–5	33	32.0
6–8	35	33.9
9+	15	14.6
Total	103	100.0

The families of the young people in the study tended to experience a range of difficulties. In 49 per cent there is known to be domestic violence, while in 52 per cent of families one or both parents are addicted to alcohol and in 8 per cent of cases one or both parents are known to abuse drugs. Over 72 per cent of young people had serious relationship difficulties with their parents and 24 per cent had difficulties with siblings.

Table 3.6: Family Difficulties

Difficulties	Number	Percentage
Relationship difficulties between young person and parent(s)	75	72.8
Alcohol addiction of parent(s)	54	52.4
Domestic violence	50	48.5
Accommodation difficulties	30	29.1
Relationship difficulties between young person and siblings	25	24.3
Severe financial difficulties	24	23.3
Mental problems of parent(s)	10	9.7
Drug abuse by parent(s)	8	7.8
Other	22	21.4

N=103

Violence in the home (including both physical violence and sexual abuse), loss of one parent through separation or death, and alcohol and drug addiction of parents create severe trauma, grief and loss for young people. Given the violence within the families and other environmental factors, it is not surprising that a high percentage of young people in the study exhibit a range of difficulties, including disruptive behaviour (82 per cent), delayed learning as a result of irregular school attendance (81 per cent), irregular school attendance (92 per cent), misuse of drugs (50 per cent) and alcohol (30 per cent), and involvement in crime (85 per cent).[4]

Eighteen per cent of young people were suspected of being sexually abused. There were six young people who displayed inappropriate sexual behaviour or had a tendency towards being sexual abusers. Table 3.7 summarises the range of difficulties experienced by young people.

---

[4] These findings illustrate a similar level of trauma to that experienced by young people in special schools studied by Fahy-Bates (1996). That study found that the majority of young people came from families who were unemployed (65 per cent). Where parents were employed, they tended to be in casual, unskilled labouring work. Twenty-seven per cent of mothers had suffered from a psychiatric illness, usually depression. Trauma such as being involved in a car crash or witnessing a drowning, a fire, suicide or murder had occurred in the lives of 65 per cent of young people. Forty-five per cent were out of home on a temporary or permanent basis at some stage during their lives. Sixty-one per cent came from a family where some members had been involved in crime. Physical violence was a factor in 71 per cent of homes. Fifty-eight per cent had experienced or were suspected of experiencing physical violence. Twenty-four per cent had been sexually abused or were suspected of being sexually abused. Only 16 per cent of young people were regular school attenders and 58 per cent had been suspended from school at least once. Only 1 per cent had a reading age appropriate to their chronological age and spelling ages and maths ages were four to five years lower than average.

Table 3.7: Young People's Own Difficulties

Difficulties	Number	Percentage
Has been an irregular school attender	95	92.2
Is known to be involved in criminal activity	87	84.5
Displays socially disruptive behaviour	84	81.6
Has delayed learning (due to irregular school attendance)	83	80.6
Has a problem with drugs, solvents or glue	51	49.5
Has a problem with alcohol	30	29.1
Has been or is suspected of having been sexually abused	19	18.4
Has a gambling problem	4	3.9

N=103

Twenty-three per cent (24) of young people were identified as having a special need and three young people had more than one special need. Special needs included physical disability (5), learning disability, i.e. mental handicap (13), and mental health problems (9).

Reasons for Placement

The majority of young people come from areas where there is a high level of disadvantage and where criminal behaviour and drug use are widespread. The factors identified by staff as directly contributing to the young person being placed in care are shown in Table 3.8. Along with the young person's criminal behaviour, which was an important factor for 80 per cent of young people being placed in special schools, the young person being out of control, parental disharmony and the parents' misuse of alcohol were also important contributory factors.

Table 3.8: Factors Contributing to Young Person Being Placed in Care

Difficulties	Number	Percentage
Criminal behaviour of young person	83	80.6
Young person out of control	35	34.0
Parental disharmony	16	15.5
Parent(s) abuse of alcohol	15	14.6
Young person at risk of emotional abuse	9	8.7
Young person at risk of physical neglect	7	6.8
Parents incapable of caring for the young person	5	4.9
Young person at risk of physical abuse	4	3.9
Young person at risk of sexual abuse	4	3.9
Parents' abuse of drugs	4	3.9
Young person abandoned	1	1.0

N=103

Care History and Placements

The majority of the young people were in special schools because they were convicted of a criminal offence (68.9). The following cases illustrate how young people enter special schools as a result of criminal activity:

> *Michael,* who is 16 years old and has nine siblings, has been misusing drugs over a number of years and his criminal behaviour is strongly linked to his drug use. He has been involved in burglaries, larcenies and a bank robbery to get money for drugs. He has over 100 outstanding charges. Michael's father died when Michael was very young, and he is still suffering the effects of this bereavement. He has a good relationship with his mother. He lives in an area where un-

employment and the related problems of crime and drug misuse are widespread. His younger brother is also in a special school, and four of his older brothers are drug addicts and have spent time in prison. He was first placed in a special school for two years when he was nine years old and has since been admitted to special schools three times.

Gary comes from an area where there are high levels of inter-generational unemployment. He achieved status in the area as a result of his ability to steal and drive fast cars. He is addicted to the buzz that goes with joy-riding, the ramming of cars and the chase by the gardaí. His mother and father are both chronic alcoholics. Gary's family has been evicted from their local authority house because of Gary's anti-social behaviour. One of his brothers is in a special school. Other brothers are serious drug users. Gary has numerous outstanding charges. He reoffended while out on leave from the special school and has been readmitted.

However, a significant proportion of young people in St. Laurence's and St. Joseph's are placed for non-attendance at school (19.4 percent) and by health boards under care orders (11.7 per cent):

Jim comes from an area where there is a high level of unemployment. His father is unemployed and there are five children in the family. The stress of poverty is aggravated by his father's drink problem. Jim was an irregular school attendee and was committed to a special school when he was 14 years of age, for non-attendance at school. He had not been involved in crime. While in the special school, he disclosed that two men had sexually abused him. The trauma resulting from this abuse was a major factor in his non-attendance at school.

Jason's mother is suffering from manic depression. His father is a heavy drinker and Jason had major difficulties in relating to him. Jason left home on several occasions and ended up living rough on the streets and in squats. As the family situation deteriorated, Jason was placed in care under a voluntary agreement between the health board and the family. His placement in a special school was primarily a result of homelessness.

Interviews with young people indicated that the response of staff in general and in particular the personal attention given by the key workers were important to them. They also appreciated that their level of education improved while in the special school:

> "St. Laurence's was great. There is a key-worker. You know you have a friend."

> "Joseph's was great. It was in St. Joseph's that I learned to read and write. It's where I got my education. We spent the summers in Waterford. It was great fun. We got everything we wanted."

> "I liked Trinity House. It was like a hotel. I got phone calls each day. The school was good, there was a gym and the staff were good."

Although young people talked positively about their time in St. Joseph's, the long distance from Dublin created difficulties for some young people from Dublin:

> "I missed Dublin, the city lights and cars. We had to steal cars to get away from Clonmel. It was boring during the winter. I did not like the mountains and hills."

Young people often derive a special status in the community from having been in a special school. They often, however, feel blamed, labelled and excluded:

> "My friends' mas say, 'keep away from him'. I'm always blamed if there is trouble, even when I am working and not where the trouble is."

Only 17 per cent of young people in the study had never been in care before their current admission. For 52 per cent it was their second admission and for 22 per cent it was their third care placement. Nine per cent had four or more admissions. Just under a quarter (25) had been in the care of a health board as well as a special school.

Table 3.9 illustrates the legal status of the 103 young people in the study population.

Table 3.9: Legal Status on Entering Special Schools

Status	Number	Percentage
Court order for criminal behaviour	70	67.6
Court order for non-attendance at school	20	19.5
Voluntary agreement between parents and health board	13	12.9
Total	103	100.0

Fifteen per cent first entered care under 10 years of age and 27 per cent entered care between the ages of 11 and 13. The majority (58 per cent) entered care between the ages of 14 and 16.

Table 3.10: Age Entered Care

Years	Number	Percentage
5 or under	2	1.9
6–10	13	12.6
11–13	28	27.2
14–16	60	58.3
Total	103	100.0

Only 11 per cent of young people in the study had been in care for less than a year. Over 53 per cent had been in care for between one and two years. A quarter had been in care for between two and five years.

Table 3.11: Time Spent in Care

Months/Years	Number	Percentage
Less than 6 months	2	1.9
6–11 months	9	8.7
1–2 years	55	53.4
2–5 years	26	25.3
5+ years	11	10.7
Total	103	100.0

Geographical Backgrounds

Young people in the special schools come from all over the country, but the highest number (44) are from Dublin (see Table 3.12).

Table 3.12: Home Base by County

County	St. Joseph's	St. Laurence's	OBC	Trinity House	OGC	Total
Leinster						
Dublin	15	11	7	10	1	44
Kildare				1		1
Kilkenny	2			1		3
Longford	1					1
Louth			3			3
Meath	1					1
Offaly	1					1
Westmeath				1		1
Wexford			1	1		2
Wicklow		1				1
Munster						
Clare	2					2
Cork		4	3	4	2	13
Limerick		1		1	1	3
Tipperary	2			2		4
Waterford	2		2			4
Connacht						
Galway	1			4	1	6
Mayo	1					1
Ulster						
Cavan	1		2			3
Donegal	1			2		3
No fixed abode			2			2
Other state			1			1
No information	1	2				3
Total	31	19	21	27	5	103

Approximately 10 per cent of the young people in the study did not have visits from parents, and a further 10 per cent had visits less often than every six months. Thirty-one per cent had weekly visits and 40 per cent monthly visits. Visits in this context means either the young person visiting their parent(s) or the parent(s) visiting the young person.

In 44 per cent of cases there were difficulties regarding visits. The main difficulty perceived by staff in arranging visits between the young person and his or her parents was the distance of the special school from home (18 per cent). This is not surprising, given that the home base of 60 per cent of the young people is over 40 miles away from the special school (see Table 3.13). Other factors were lack of parental interest (15 per cent) and fears for the young person because of a destructive relationship between him or her and the parent(s) (13 per cent). The fact that so many young people do have regular contact with their parents reflects both the interests of parents and the time and energy given by staff in special schools in arranging these visits.

Table 3.13: *Distance of Special School from Home*

Distance from home	Number	Percentage
Under 1 mile	2	1.9
1–5 miles	9	8.7
9–19 miles	22	21.4
20–40 miles	8	7.8
More than 40 miles	62	60.2
Total	103	100.0

While in special school, 22 per cent of young people were visited by a health board social worker. Visits were mainly made to young people who were in special schools for not attending school and who were placed by the health board under a voluntary care order.

Misplacements

Twenty-three per cent (21) of the young people surveyed were considered by staff to be inappropriately placed. It was felt that some young people who were in secure units could be transferred to a more open centre or a halfway hostel. The need for short-stay specialised units for young people with addiction problems was identified. Three young people needed a residential centre that could respond to the specific challenges of mental handicap and four young people needed a service which responded to the cultural needs of the Travelling community. The following cases illustrate examples of inappropriate placements:

> *Mike* was committed to a special school for non-attendance at school. While in school he disclosed that a neighbour had abused him. His father could not deal with the abuse issue and tended to blame his son for being abused. His brothers call him a "queer". The school referred Mike to counselling to address the abuse issue and to help him build his self-esteem. There was a long waiting list for counselling and when his time finally came, he did not attend. Staff are of the opinion that Mike should not be in the same unit as young people who have a history of persistent criminal activity. He needs a service that would help him to deal with his abuse. He craves positive attention and acceptance and needs a lot of support in order to learn not to blame himself for the abuse.

> *Gerry* lives in an area where drugs are widespread. He became involved with drugs when he was 12 years of age. He was also involved in petty crime in order to fund his drug problem. He was committed to a secure unit at the age of 14 for two years for receiving stolen goods worth £10. Staff are of the opinion that Gerry should not have been placed in a secure unit. He is a drug addict, not a criminal.

> *Sean* was 13 years old when he was first placed in a special school for young offenders for non-attendance at school. His father has a problem with alcohol. He is a domineering man and aggressive towards Sean's mother. At 15, Sean was convicted of larceny and committed to a special school. He

alleged that a neighbour sexually abused him. While in the school he attended a child sexual abuse treatment unit in the Regional Hospital. The Community Care services investigated the abuse, but the case was not resolved. Sean was distressed that the case could not be resolved and developed a problem with alcohol. While in the school, he was abusive and bullied other young people. Staff felt that he was misplaced in a reformatory. He needed a therapeutic placement to help him deal with issues of sexual abuse and addiction.

These examples illustrate the need for a range of placement options for young people whose primary issue is not criminal behaviour. Options should include residential homes, therapeutic units and units that can cater for young people with special needs. The practice of mixing these young people whose main issue is not criminal behaviour with young people who are engaged in persistent criminal activity is a cause for concern.

The misplacement of a significant proportion of the population results from the fact that many young people are placed not on the basis of need but on the basis of which places are available. Misplacing young people in special schools is serious for many reasons. Firstly, when a young person is placed in a special school his or her movements are severely restricted and he or she is deprived of the day-to-day responsibility of managing his own life. If unjustly placed, the young person can be extremely angry and aggrieved. Secondly, maintaining a young person in a special school is expensive. Thirdly, misplacement deprives other people in need of the placement.

Misplacement also indicates a lack of flexibility in the system in responding to the changing needs of young people. After a period in a special school the needs of the young person may require that he or she be transferred to a more open environment in the community or in foster care. To achieve this special schools need greater flexibility and to have access to a range of options, including health board-type facilities. The current fragmentation of responsibilities between the Department of Education and Science and the Department of Health and Children does not facilitate these arrangements.

Reviews and Care Plans

Since the early 1990s, it is the practice of all special schools to develop care plans for the young people in their care. The great majority (85 per cent) of care plans were reviewed every six months or more frequently. Considerable effort is made to encourage parents to have an input into the care plan.

Specific issues needing to be addressed by the young person are identified by care staff and become part of the care plan. The following are the range of issues included in care plans:

- Anger management

- Violent behaviour

- Self-esteem

- Social skills

- Relationships with family

- Educational support

- Bereavement

- Sex education

- Alcohol and drug misuse

- Criminal behaviour.

Each young person is assigned a key-worker, who develops a relationship with the young person and helps him or her to address the issues outlined in the care plan. Key-workers thus play a central role in the care system by providing intensive support to the young person.

In addition, 68 per cent of young people were referred to special services, such as counselling, and psychological services. Three of the five special schools have a resident psychologist to support staff and young people, while two special schools contract in the counselling and psychological skills they require. In addition, for specific issues such as addiction or sexual abuse, young people are linked to specialist services where possible. It was noted in particular that there is a lack of detoxification facilities for young people. Also, it was not always possible to get access to appropriate therapeutic counselling when needed.

For the most part, it is the practice to invite parents and young people to attend review meetings. In relation to the last review before the young person left care, 91 per cent of parents were invited to attend it and 53 per cent did attend. The reasons for parents not attending included distance from the special school, responsibility for younger children and, in a minority of cases, lack of interest. Nearly 70 per cent of parents had some input into the last review meeting, either by attending the review in person or through phone contact between parents and key-workers or through visits to the parents in their homes by staff.

Schools recognise the importance of parental involvement if the young person is to return home and stay out of crime. They encourage the participation of parents in a variety of ways. One school is organising a parenting course, involving structured group discussions in the school. Parents are offered free transport to attend the course.

In some cases, where parents have long distances to travel in order to visit their children, they are facilitated to stay overnight, and staff formally engage visiting parents in discussion on the circumstances, difficulties and plans for the young people.

Another school has established a parents' group for parents in the Dublin area. They meet once a week and the group is facilitated by staff of the special school and staff of the Probation and Welfare Service.

The general point was made that, while schools make enormous efforts to involve parents, they have no specific resources to employ outreach and family workers to develop their work with parents. Also, the long distances between school and home make this work very difficult.

In relation to young people's own participation in their care plans, 90 per cent were invited to attend the last review meeting before they left care, and 75 per cent attended. Some young people chose not to attend because of nervousness or shyness and some asked their key-workers to represent their views. Other young people were not at review meetings because they had absconded.

The satisfaction of young people with review meetings needs to be further explored. A study in Northern Ireland (Horgan, 1996) suggests that young people are ill-prepared for review meetings and that their voice is not being adequately heard at these meetings. If they are to participate in a meaningful way, the study suggests, much more preparation is required and they should also be involved in decisions about who should attend the meetings.

3.2 LEAVING CARE

Prior to entering the special schools, the vast majority of young people were irregular school attenders. While in the special schools, a great deal of attention was paid to their education. On exiting the care system, 56 per cent had taken some subjects in the Junior Certificate (Foundation Level). Thirty-nine per cent, however, had not gone beyond primary school level and 82 per cent of young people were not returning to school.

Staff were of the opinion that for 38 per cent of young people leaving the special schools there were important issues that had not been fully addressed, either because there were difficulties in engaging the young people or because appropriate services were not available.

While in a special schools, young people live in a highly structured environment. They leave care at 16 years or younger. A young person leaving a special school is unlikely to have consistent contact or support from staff in the special school.[5] There is no legislative basis or resources to enable special schools to provide an aftercare service. In the absence of resources, care workers in their own time attempt to maintain contact with the young person, and to provide aftercare sup-

---

[5] In 1998, St. Laurence's established a through-care project on its campus for boys in St. Laurence's, Kilronan Grove Project which caters for nine boys. The aim of the project is to prepare young people to live independently. Project facilities include supported accommodation, semi-supported accommodation and a bedsit.

ports. Staff of special school considered that 58 per cent of the young people leaving the schools needed an aftercare service.

Key relationships, which have developed over a period of years, come to an abrupt end when the young person leaves the special school. One key-worker explained:

> "You help them to pack their bags, take the posters down from the wall and say goodbye. You tell them to keep in contact and to ring you."

On leaving care, the majority (63 per cent) return to their families. A further 6 per cent were placed in hostel accommodation, supported lodgings or in foster homes, and the remaining 28 per cent either went to prison/special school (18 per cent) or absconded and their whereabouts were unknown (10 per cent).

Table 3.14: Destination of Young People on Leaving Care

Destination	Number	Percentage
Family/relatives	65	63.1
Placed in foster care	1	1.0
Supported lodgings	5	4.8
Hostel accommodation	3	3.0
Absconded	10	9.7
Detention centre	19	18.4
Total	103	100.0

For the young people who returned home or who were placed in other accommodation, their transition from care was planned. The key-worker engaged in extensive planning with the young people. On returning home the vast majority were either at school or work or were linked to a training course. Sixteen of the 18 young people who were still at school on leaving the special school had school placements arranged for them.

The circumstances of the family had improved for approximately 50 per cent of young people who returned home. Examples of this include parents addressing their own addiction issues, improved family understanding of the young person and in one instance, the father who had abused the young person leaving the family home. Where it is possible to engage the family, successful work can be done, as the following cases illustrate:

Michael discovered the identity of his father when he was ten years old. His father was living with his mother's cousin, whom he knew well, in a nearby neighbourhood. This caused a lot of distress for Michael. He left home and went to live with his uncle. His uncle was a heroin addict and lived a chaotic life style. While with his uncle, Michael began to use heroin. He left his uncle's flat after three months and moved in with a friend. He soon ended up living on the streets and was placed by the health board in an emergency hostel for homeless young people. He gradually became involved in a life of crime. He was placed in a special school. While in the special school, he resumed his education and passed four subjects in the Junior Certificate. The school engaged Michael and his mother in family counselling and provided individual counselling for Michael to help him to address his relationship with his natural father. Keyworkers also visited Michael's mother at home regularly and supported her to attend Alcoholic Anonymous meetings. Michael made a lot of progress while in the special school. The family circumstances have also improved significantly. Staff were hopeful that Michael would remain out of trouble with the law. However, despite the improved circumstances at home, two years later, Michael had become involved with drugs and was in prison.

Tom's father had left the family home when he was six years of age. Tom had five siblings and his mother found it difficult to cope. She also had a problem with alcohol. Two of his younger siblings were adopted. Tom had been placed in a special school for causing criminal damage to property. While in the special schools, Tom resumed his education and passed the four subjects in the Junior Certificate. Keyworkers also supported Tom's mother and arranged transport for her to visit Tom regularly in the special school. She lived in very poor accommodation and they supported her to move into new accommodation. Tom and his mother attended counselling sessions with a family therapist, and Tom also attended individual counselling sessions. The key-worker made arrangements for Tom to attend a community-based youth project for early school leavers, and supported Tom to stay in the project. Two years later Tom was still living at home and attending the training course.

For 50 per cent of the young people studied, there was no improvement in family circumstances. In some cases, it was felt that returning home was not the most advisable course of action. However, in the absence of suitable alternative accommodation many young people were forced to return to extremely difficult home circumstances, as the following examples illustrate:

John was sexually abused by his father. John's father was also violent to his mother. His mother found it difficult to cope and four of his siblings were taken into care. John was placed in a special school as a result of joy-riding activities. Staff feel that a therapeutic placement would have been a better response to John's needs than a special school. On the completion of his placement at 16 years of age, staff identified the need for him to be placed in supported lodgings. Staff failed to get the health board to arrange supported lodgings, so John returned home to a very difficult situation. The sexual abuse issue had not been resolved and on his discharge, there was no clear decision relating to the respective roles of the health board and special schools. John left home a number of months later and went to live with his sister. He became involved in drugs. Two years later he was in prison for larceny.

Darren's dad died when he was 12 years of age. His mother established a new relationship. Darren rejected his mother's new partner. While in the special school he exhibited extreme anger towards his mother. He had nowhere to go when discharged from the special school at the age of 15. His two brothers were in prison. He did not want to return to his mother's house and his mother's partner did not want him there either. In the absence of the availability of supported lodgings, Darren returned home. He became involved in crime and two years later was in prison.

Donal's father is a drug addict and a major drug dealer. His father left the family home and soon after was sentenced to prison in England. Donal felt rejected by his mother, who is vulnerable and finds it difficult to cope. She had rent arrears with the local authority and was evicted from her local authority house. One of Donal's brothers is also in a special school. Donal is a heroin addict and while in the special school received addiction counselling. He also came to terms with the fact that he could not rely on his mother or father. Donal's mother is living with another partner and staff were of the opinion that it was not suitable for Donal to return home. They failed to acquire suitable supported accommodation for him, however, and he therefore returned home. Several months later he left home and was homeless. He became involved in crime and was committed to prison. On release from prison he returned home. He needs therapeutic help to cope with depression and addiction and needs supported accommodation.

These examples show that for some young people, the family difficulties associated with the young person being placed in care in the first place were not resolved on leaving care.

The following is an example of a young person who on discharge had nowhere to go and was placed in hostel accommodation, which was inappropriate:

Declan's father had received a long-term prison sentence for a violent crime. His mother was unable to cope. At the age of three, the health board placed Declan in a residential unit. He was in and out of care and had a total of nine placements. While in care he disclosed that his father had sexually abused him. His father had also been charged with sexually abusing his sister. His mother had developed a problem with alcohol, was unable to pay her rent and ended up in hostels for homeless women. Declan also ended up homeless and engaged in petty crime. He became involved in prostitution. He was convicted of assault. The person who he assaulted was a well-known paedophile. He was placed in care. A lot of work was undertaken with Declan while in the special school. He received individual counselling for sexual abuse and undertook specific programmes on social skills. There was concern, however, that Declan was a potential abuser, as he displayed inappropriate sexual behaviour. On being discharged from the special school, Declan had nowhere to go. The special school made the case to the health board that Declan needed a small, safe, specialised residential unit, which was highly staffed. They were concerned that he would abuse other young people or emulate his father's violent behaviour. The health board placed him in an inner city emergency hostel, which left him open to the drift of inner city street life. He was also in an environment which left him open to being sexually abused himself or sexually abusing others. The special school considered this to be a totally inappropriate placement.

3.3 FOLLOW-UP: SIX MONTHS AND TWO YEARS ON

Six months after leaving care, 91 per cent (94) of the original 103 young people were tracked, one of whom had died as a result of a drug overdose. Nine young people were not tracked. These included three young people who were in England. The whereabouts of the remaining six were not known.

Two years after leaving care, 88 per cent (91) of the original population of 103 young people were tracked.

While none of the young people were parents on leaving care, three of the five girls had given birth to a child and 13 males had fathered children two years after leaving care.

Table 3.15 shows the living arrangements of the special school population on leaving care, six months after leaving care and two years after leaving care.

Six months after leaving care, the numbers of young people living with family or relatives had decreased from 63 per cent (65) to 48 per cent (45). Two years after leaving care the percentage living with family or relatives had decreased to 45 per cent (40).

Table 3.15: Living Arrangements of Care Leavers on Leaving Care, Six Months and Two Years After Leaving Special Schools

Living Arrangements	On Leaving Care (%)	6 Months On (%)	2 Years On (%)
Family and relatives	63.1	48.3	40.7
Prison/detention centre	18.4	38.7	46.2
Living independently, private rented sector	0.0	2.1	1.1
Probation hostel	3.0	3.3	1.1
Supported lodgings/homeless	4.8	2.2	5.5
Deceased	0.0	1.1	1.1
Foster family	1.0	1.1	0.0
Absconded	9.7	0.0	0.0
Other	0.0	3.2	4.3
Total percentage	100.0	100.0	100.0
N	103	93	91

Detention

Many of the young people who were not residing with their family were in prison. The total number of special school leavers who were in a place of detention or prison had more than doubled from 18 per cent (19) on leaving care to 39 per cent (36) six months later. A further 12 young people had been in a place of detention at some stage during the six months since leaving care. This means that 48 (51 per cent) had been in detention at some time during the six-month period after leaving care.

Two years after leaving care, 46 per cent (42) of young people were in a place of detention or prison. An additional 17 young people had been sentenced to a placement of detention or to prison during the two-year period, bringing the number identified who had spent time in detention to 59. This means that 65 per cent of the special school population who had been tracked had been in a place of detention or prison at some time during the two-year period after leaving care. A further seven had been sentenced by the courts at some stage during the two years, but not sent to prison.

A special search was undertaken of the prison records at the end of 1999, which for some young people was three years after leaving care. This search revealed that 63 per cent (65 young people) of the total population of 103 young people had been to a place of detention or adult prison. A further three young people had been returned to a special school. This means that 66 per cent (68) had been to either a special school, place of detention or adult prison after leaving care.[6] Many of the young people had been in detention multiple times.

The percentage suspected of being involved in crime had decreased from 83 per cent six months after leaving care to 78 per cent two years after leaving care.

Young people in the study population were committed to prison for a variety of reasons, such as larceny, joy-riding and assault. At least one young person was committed for murder and several were committed for grievous bodily harm. Young people interviewed for the study described their attitudes towards crime and life in prison:

> "If I see money, I just have to have it. I just would not leave it there. Money is very important to me. I don't know why."

> "I have been locked up most of my life. I was in Laurence's and Trinity. I am doing time for robbing. It is the fastest way of getting money."

All experienced prison as severe:

> "It's an absolute nightmare. You don't know who to trust. You're locked up for 18 hours a day in Pat's. I don't like

---

[6] A special search was undertaken of prison records to derive this figure.

Pat's. Staff are different here than in Trinity. They don't really care about you here."

"Pat's is worse than Mountjoy. It is a dump. You cannot go anywhere without the doors locking behind you. There are flies in the food. You can't eat it."

"Prisoners have no rights. There is no respect for prisoners. You have to wear prison clothes and you are not allowed a television in your room. The guards here slag you about being a junkie and threaten to send you to Spike."

"The thing I miss most in prison is my ma."

On leaving prison there is little preparation for living in the outside world:

"There is no preparation, no notice. One morning you are told, 'right you, you are going home. Pack your stuff'. You may have no money and nowhere to go. It doesn't even matter if you are on a treatment programme."

Their views of their future were bleak. Many of the young people expressed total hopelessness:

"I don't know where I will go, maybe I can stay with my sister."

"I am not really looking forward to coming out. There is nothing out there. It is hard to keep out of trouble. You're in the snooker hall all day and go out and rob."

"If I don't have a job and money I will drift into trouble."

"When I leave I know that I will get involved again in drugs."

It is the exceptional young person who was hopeful:

"I miss my ma and da here. I hated school, but I have always worked. When I get out I will get a job. I also have a motor bike and a girlfriend."

Work

The work status of the young people reflected the early age at which they left school and their low level of educational achievement. Sixty per cent (62) left school at 15 years or younger and 21 per cent left without any qualifications. Table 3.16 shows the work status of the young people two years after leaving special schools.

Table 3.16: Work Status of Young People Six Months and Two Years After Leaving Special Schools

Work status	6 Months On (N)	%	2 Years On (N)	%
Place of detention/adult prison	36	38.7	36	39.5
Unemployed	19	20.4	11	12.1
On Youthreach/community training workshop/training course	19	20.4	8	8.8
Employed	14	15.1	18	19.8
At school	4	4.3	1	1.1
In further education	1	1.1	1	1.1
Home duties	0	0.0	3	3.3
No information	0	0	13	14.3
Total	93	100	91	100.0

Of the 93 young people tracked six months after leaving care, 15 per cent (14) were employed and six had an income in excess of £100 a week. Of the 19 who were unemployed, ten were dependent on their family for income.

Two years after leaving care, the numbers in work increased from 15 per cent to 20 per cent. Correspondingly, the numbers of unemployed and on Youthreach and community training programmes had decreased. This reflects the increasing buoyancy and the phenomenal growth of the Irish economy. The economy is now entering a phase where there is a skills shortage in many sectors. Marginalised youth, which include ex-offenders, are now being offered employment if they can prove that they are sufficiently stable to hold down a job.

Many of the jobs that are accessible, however, are low skilled, low paid with little prospects of promotion. In this new economic climate, the challenge is to support young people to remain in employment and to support them to up-skill in order to avail of enhanced labour market opportunities. An aftercare support service inter-linked to community-based service, as outlined in the recommendations of this study, is central to helping care leavers to avail of such opportunities.

Three of the five young girls had given birth who were engaged in home duties.

Networks of Support

Six months after leaving care, 77 per cent (72) had the support of a family member. The percentage of young people with support from a family member decreased to 60 per cent (55) two years after leaving care. Significantly, for over 47 per cent (43) of young people the relationship between the young person and family was described as a good relationship. For 15 per cent (14) of young people contact with family was very infrequent, being less often once a month.

Special schools do not have the resources or legislative basis to provide aftercare for young people leaving care. It is not surprising that two years after leaving care, only 6 per cent (5) had frequent contact with the special school, although 30 per cent (28) of young people had some contact. For over 58 per cent (53) there had been no contact in the previous 18 months.[7]

Two years after leaving care eight young people were getting support from special youth projects and two young people were getting support from a voluntary agency.

As was expected, a large percentage (62 per cent) had contact with the Probation and Welfare Service six months after leaving care. This contact was concerned with supervision of the young people as a result of being admitted to prison,

---

[7] Young people under the age of 15 who return home to an area where the School Attendance Service operates (parts of Dublin City, Waterford City and Cork City) get support from the service.

charged with new offences or being "out on license" from the special schools. Of the 58 young people in contact with the Probation and Welfare Service, 38 per cent (22) had weekly contact, 55 per cent (32) had monthly contact and 7 per cent (4) had contact less often than once a month. The percentage of young people who had contact with the probation and welfare service decreased to 40 per cent (36) of young people two years after leaving care.

Nearly 20 per cent of the young people had contact with the Community Care social work service six months after leaving care. This contact decreased to 15 per cent (14) two years after leaving care. The contact was for the most part a result of the social worker having contact with the family on issues relating to child protection. It was rarely directly concerned with support for the young person who had left a special school. Contact made with the family tended to be on a monthly basis.

Only 21 per cent (20) of young people six months after leaving care and 10 per cent (9) of young people two years after leaving care were considered to have the appropriate level of help they needed. At the other end of the scale, the numbers of young people with little or no support from any source increased from 15 per cent (14) six months after leaving care to 32 per cent (29) two years after leaving care.

The importance of aftercare was stressed by one worker who stated that many young people lack the supports to live outside of an institutionalised environment:

> "Some young people when they are discharged lack supports and reoffend to get back into the system (i.e. to get support). If proper aftercare and specialist programmes were provided, the numbers coming back into the system would be reduced."

Difficulties

Six months after leaving care, the young people in the study experienced a range of difficulties. Thirty-two per cent (30) had difficulties with accommodation and 30 per cent (28) still had difficulties two years after leaving care.

Two years after leaving care, a large proportion of young people needed assistance to develop an education and training plan (52 per cent) and a work plan (63 per cent).

Other difficulties included unresolved relationship difficulties with family members, which was the situation for 67 per cent (61) of young people.

Two years after leaving care 43 per cent (39) of young people were known to have an addiction problem. Seven young people had taken part in a rehabilitation programme. The main types of addictions which young people were coping with are shown in Table 3.17.

Table 3.17: Addictions of Young People Two Years After Leaving Care

Types of substance	Number
Alcohol	24
Cannabis	16
Ecstasy/LSD	11
Opiates	10
Glue	3
Prescribed medicine	2
Methadone	1

N = 39

At least 30 per cent (28) of young people had experienced homelessness during the six-month period since leaving care. This figure increased to 33 per cent (30) two years after leaving care. Factors relating to the young person's homelessness included the family being unable to tolerate the young person's drug abuse, vigilantes threatening the young person because of involvement in drugs, the young person on the run from the gardai because of involvement in crime and the young person leaving home because of relationship difficulties at home. In three cases, the family of the young person was homeless.

Three young people were suspected of being involved in prostitution.

Supports Needed

Two years after leaving care staff felt that 76 per cent (69) of young people were not getting the help they needed. The following table lists the supports that staff identified as being needed by young people two years after they had left the special school.

Table 3.18: Specialists Services Needed by Care Leavers Two Years After Leaving Care

Services Needed	Number	Percentage
Intensive probation supervision	43	47.3
Counselling (general)	38	41.8
Drug rehabilitation	28	30.8
Aftercare	27	29.6
Mentor service	26	28.6
Supported accommodation	14	15.4
Specialist youth project	12	13.2
Counselling for sexual abuse	11	12.1
Culturally appropriate Traveller service	6	6.6
High-support unit	4	4.4

N = 69

The help the young people needed was a community-based intensive probation supervision programme to help young people to come to terms with their criminal behaviour (47 per cent), an aftercare service (30 per cent) and other specialist services such as counselling (42 per cent) and addiction treatment services (31 per cent).

Secure, safe accommodation was needed by 15 per cent (14) of young people and four other young people needed high-support accommodation.

Six of the 12 Travellers had severe difficulties making the transition from the special school and a special project for Travellers was needed to respond to their needs.

The following chapter examines the circumstances of young people leaving health board care and contrasts health board care leavers with young people discharged from special schools.

4

Young People Leaving
Health Board Care

"There is no aftercare policy or structure for delivering aftercare. There is the pressure of the caseload, which prioritises children up to 18 years. It depends on the manager as to whether or not you can keep on the case. He is not a priority. He is nearly 18 years and preference is given to younger, less streetwise kids. He needs a semi-independent living situation, but there is no place available." — Community Care Social Worker

Three health board regions were included in the research:

- The Eastern Health Board

- The North-Eastern Health Board

- The North-Western Health Board.

The health board study population is defined as follows:

- Young people 13 years or older in foster care, residential care, supported lodgings or semi-independent living arrangements in the three health board regions listed above, and who were discharged from care between April 1997 and September 1997.

Over the two-year research period, social workers filled out three forms on each of the young people leaving health board care. The first form concerned the characteristics and circumstances of the young people, the second form concerned their

situation six months after leaving care and the third concerned
their situation two years after leaving care.

Six months after leaving health board care 87 per cent (49) of
the original population of 56 young people were tracked and
two years after leaving care 79 per cent (44) young people
were tracked.

The methodologies for identifying the research population,
for filling out forms on these young people and for tracking the
young people are outlined in section 2.5 of this report.

With the co-operation of social workers, residential care
workers and community activists, the researchers constructed
case histories on over 20 young people. Personal interviews
were also held with 20 young people who had left health board
care.

The researchers wish to acknowledge the time and energy
given by residential care staff and social workers to tracking
young people after they had left care, which in some cases was
extremely difficult.

4.1 HEALTH BOARDS AND CARE

The Department of Health and Children and the health boards
are charged with the obligation to promote the welfare of children and to support them to live with their families where possible. Children are to be taken into care only as a last resort,
when their families are unable to care for them or when they
are at risk of neglect or abuse. In this respect, health boards are
obliged to develop community-based preventive strategies[1] in
areas where there are high levels of disadvantage. There is an
increasing emphasis on providing direct support to families
and an additional £32 million nationally is being made available
for child care service nationally.

Health boards acknowledge that their resources are insufficient and that additional resources for prevention are necessary. There is evidence that in the Eastern Health Board region
there is little time for staff to devote to development and pre-

---

[1] The obligation on health boards to develop preventive services is clearly
outlined in Section 3 of the *Child Care Act, 1991*.

ventive work, as the services are crisis-driven, with priority given to protection work (Tutt, 1997).

There has been a gradual shift from residential care to foster care over the second half of the 20th century and foster care is now firmly established as the most important source of alternative family care for children. Notwithstanding this, the provision of residential care placements is important for young people for whom foster care is not suitable. Foster care may not always be appropriate for young people whose foster care placements have broken down and young people coming into care in their teenage years. Many of these young people have experienced severe trauma and can exhibit challenging behaviour which foster-carers find difficult to deal with. Siblings coming into care who wish to remain together may also not be suitable for foster care.

The number of young people in the care of health boards at any one time is approximately 4,000. Almost 80 per cent of placements are foster care placements, of which 16 per cent are with relatives. Thirteen per cent of children in care are in residential care, 3 per cent are in care at home and 3 per cent are in "other" accommodation, such as supported lodgings and with emergency carers. Placement with relatives is becoming an increasing trend in all health board areas and there is an increasing trend to recruit relatives to undertake foster care. Placing children with relatives is believed to be less traumatic than placing children with strangers (see Table 4.1).

The principal reasons for admission to care are parents unable to cope (27 per cent), neglect (27 per cent) and parents addiction (15 per cent). Other reasons include physical abuse, sexual abuse, if a young person is out of control and if a child is abandoned.

Statistics on the length of time children are in care are not available for 1998. Figures for 1996 indicate that nearly 80 per cent of young people who are in care at any one particular time have been in care for one year or over. Forty per cent have been in care for five years or over and almost 20 per cent have been in care for ten years or over.

Table 4.1: Type of Care Provided by Health Boards, 31 December 1998

Health Board	Foster Care	Foster Care with Relatives	Residential Care	At Home under Supervision	Other	Pre-adoptive Placement	Total
Eastern	833	262	297	46	113	3	1554
Midland	168	50	22	14	0	9	263
Mid-Western	299	49	23	22	4	11	408
North-Eastern	292	52	20	3	0	3	370
North-Western	144	40	12	2	0	1	199
South-Eastern	268	55	59	2	0	4	388
Southern	383	89	57	0	9	0	538
Western	140	38	44	32	2	8	264
Total	2,527	635	534	121	128	39	3,984
Percentage	63.5	15.9	13.4	3.1	3.2	.99	100.0

Source: Department of Health and Children, 1998

The number of young people leaving the care of health boards in the country as a whole rose from 1,043 in 1992 to 1,754 in 1996,[2] an increase of 711 or 68 per cent. It is not clear why there was such an increase in numbers discharged.

All three health boards that are part of the present study are of the opinion that an increasing number of children coming into the care system are displaying difficult and challenging behaviour. Foster care is becoming increasingly demanding on carers and a growing number of health boards are contracting the Irish Foster Care Association (IFCA) to train foster-carers on the complex issues involved in foster care.

The establishment in 1981 of the Irish Foster Care Association reflects the important role which foster care is playing in the care system. The IFCA has 28 affiliated branches nationwide (Whelan, 1997). The association provides a telephone helpline for foster-carers, sends out information to prospective foster-carers, is an advisory body to the government and has bi-annual meetings with the Department of Health and Children. It negotiates with the department and the health boards on issues such as allowances, children with special needs in foster care, respite care, discretionary payments and training. In July 1993, it hosted an International Conference on Fostering in Dublin. In 1997, the government made a decision to grant-aid the Irish Foster-carers Association.[3] In 1998, the Minister of State at the Department of Health and Children established a working group on foster care, on which the Irish Foster Care Association is represented.

The need for aftercare support for young people leaving foster care has long been recognised by the Irish Foster Care Association.[4] It was a major theme of their 1997 annual conference. The Association has emphasised the importance of care planning in order to provide the young person and the foster-carers with real choices when the young person reaches 18

---

[2] Statistics are not available for 1998.

[3] The IFCA has published several important publications, including *Fostering Care* (leaflet); *A Journey Through Fostering*, 1995;and *Grieving the Children* (by Anne McWilliams).

[4] North-Eastern Health Board, *Review of Child Care and Family Support Services,* 1996.

years. The point was made that where there is no leaving care plan, health boards often presume that foster-carers will continue to support the young person. The association points to the need for consultation with all interested parties. Health boards should also take a proactive role in accessing independent accommodation for the young person leaving foster care placements and in assisting the young person to settle into their new accommodation.

Notwithstanding the wide promotion and endorsement of foster care, health boards are encountering difficulties recruiting sufficient foster-carers to meet demand. McWilliams (1997) and Whelan (1997) outline some of these difficulties, as follows:

- Lack of recognition of the complex role of foster-carers
- Low level of payment received by foster-carers for placements
- Challenging behaviour of many young people
- Fear of allegations of sexual, physical or emotional abuse
- Expectation that there will be increasing contact between children and birth parents, and the complexity that this can involve
- Lack of pre-service training
- Lack of support and post-placement training for foster-carers
- Need for 24-hour service to support foster placements
- Contracting supply of foster mothers, due to increasing numbers of women entering the labour market.

In addition, there is a need for increased access for foster-carers to respite care, particularly for families who are fostering children with challenging behaviour.

An outline of the care system in the three health board regions is provided in Appendix 2.

4.2 FINDINGS: YOUNG PEOPLE LEAVING HEALTH BOARD CARE

The Study Population

Table 4.2 outlines the numbers of young people leaving care in the three health board regions.

Table 4.2: Number of Young People Leaving Care in the Study Area, During the Study Period

Health Board Region	Number
1. Dún Laoghaire	7
2. Dublin South East	0
3. Dublin South Central	2
4. Dublin South West	5
5. Dublin West	1
6, Dublin North West	2
7. Dublin North Central	7
8. Dublin North	6
9. Kildare	2
10. Wicklow	4
Eastern Health Board	**36**
Cavan/Monaghan	4
Louth	3
Meath	7
North-Eastern Health Board	**14**
Donegal	2
Sligo/Leitrim	4
North-Western Health Board	**6**
Total	**56**

The number leaving care in the three health board areas who were 13 years or older was 56. This number is less than expected. It is far below the number (110) identified in a recent

Northern Ireland study (Pinkerton and Ross, 1996) as having left Department of Health care over a six-month period. Northern Ireland has a population of only 1.5 million, compared to the population of over 2 million in the three health board regions under study.

This figure for young people leaving health board care is probably an underestimate. In the absence of a database or records on young people leaving care in the EHB area,[5] it is impossible to arrive at an accurate figure. This in turn makes it difficult for the social work service to plan an adequate response to the needs of young people leaving care.

The characteristics of the leaving-care population of the three health board regions are outlined in the next tables.

Table 4.3: Leaving Care Population by Sex

Sex	Number	Percentage
Male	28	50.0
Female	28	50.0
Total	56	100.0

Table 4.4: Age on Leaving Care

Age	Number	Percentage
13 to 14 years	3	5.4
15 to 16 years	13	23.2
17 to 18 years	27	48.2
18+	10	17.8
No information	3	5.4
Total	56	100

There were equal numbers of males and females leaving care, and most of them left care at 17 or 18 years of age.

---

[5] In only one Community Care Area in the EHB region was it possible for the social work manager to identify the number of young people leaving care.

Young people with a Traveller background made up 9 per cent (5) of the health board leaving-care population. This is slightly lower than for the special school leaving-care population, which had a Traveller population of 12 per cent.

Fifty per cent (28) have siblings who are or have been in care. This is a higher percentage than for young people in special schools, where 35 per cent had siblings who were in care.

Similar to the special school population, none of the young people had given birth or been responsible for a birth on leaving health board care.

Personal and Family Circumstances

Although young people in the care of the health boards are not a homogeneous population, reception into health board care, as with placement in a special school, is closely associated with poverty and disadvantage. The accommodation type of eight families was not known.

Table 4.5: Accommodation of Parents

Accommodation	Number	Percentage
Local authority	27	56.3
Owner-occupied	8	16.7
Private rented	4	8.3
Insecure accommodation	9	18.7
Total	48	100.0

Seventeen per cent lived in owner-occupied accommodation and 8 per cent in the private rented sector. Just over 56 per cent of parents lived in local authority accommodation and under 19 per cent of the parents (9) lived in insecure accommodation. This included one family who lived in a tent, a Traveller family who had a nomadic existence, and a mother who was a lone parent living in a psychiatric hospital. Six families, were homeless, either living in hostels or refuges or living with friends.

Just over 3 per cent of mothers and 20 per cent of fathers of the young people in the study were in full-time employment, indicating a high dependency on social welfare.

Only 39 per cent of the young people had parents who were living together and four young people had been in care since their birth, having been abandoned by their parents

Families of the young people experienced a range of difficulties. As with the special school population, high levels of family difficulties were experienced. In 80 per cent of cases there were relationship difficulties between parents and the young person. Many families also experienced alcohol addiction and mental health problems. In 50 per cent of cases (28), the young people had siblings who were also in care.

Table 4.6: Family Difficulties

Difficulties	Number	Percentage
Relationship difficulties between parent(s) and young person	45	80.4
Domestic violence	22	39.6
Alcohol addiction of parent(s)	26	46.4
Mental problems of parent(s)	17	30.4
Relationship difficulties between young person and siblings	18	32.1
Severe financial difficulties	8	14.3
Accommodation difficulties	9	16.1
Drug misuse by parent(s)	6	10.7

N = 56

In both the special school population and the health board population, high levels of domestic violence were experienced. The level of violence was 10 per cent higher in the special school population than in the health board population.

As well as family difficulties, young people in health board care experienced a similar range of difficulties as young people placed in special schools. As might be expected, young people in special schools were four times more likely to be involved in crime than the health board population. They were also more likely to be an irregular school attender and to display socially disruptive behaviour.

On the other hand, the health board population was more than twice as likely than the special school population to have been identified as being sexually abused.

Table 4.7: Young People's Own Difficulties

Difficulties	Number	Percentage
Has been an irregular school attender	29	51.8
Displays socially disruptive behaviour	25	44.6
Has been or is suspected of being sexually abused	23	41.1
Has a problem with drugs, solvents or glue	17	30.4
Has delayed learning (due to irregular school attendance)	16	28.6
Is known to be involved in criminal activity	12	21.4
Has a problem with alcohol	9	16.1
Displays inappropriate sexual behaviour	3	5.3

N = 56

Five per cent (3) of the health board population displayed inappropriate sexual behaviour or had a tendency towards being a sexual abuser. This is slightly lower than for the special schools population, which was 6 per cent (5).

Both groups had significant sub-groups with a special need. Twenty-three per cent of young people in the special school population were identified as having a special need, compared with 39 per cent (22) of the health board population. As with the special school population, five young people had more than one special need. Special needs for the health board population included mental health problems (11), learning disability, i.e. mental handicap (10), and physical disability (5). Mental health problems included clinical depression, eating disorders, suicidal tendencies and propensity to inflict self-harm.

Table 4.8 shows the factors identified by staff as contributing to the young people being taken into care.

Table 4.8: Factors Contributing to Admission to Care

Factors	Number	Percentage
At risk of physical neglect	21	37.5
At risk of physical abuse	17	30.4
At risk of sexual abuse	13	23.2
Young person abandoned	13	23.2
At risk of emotional abuse	15	26.7
Parents incapable of caring for young person	11	19.6
Young person out of control	9	16.1
Parental disharmony	8	14.2
Parents' misuse of alcohol	8	14.2
Parents' misuse of drugs	4	7.1

N = 56

Care History and Placements

The following tables outlines the type of care placement of young people at the time of leaving care. A large proportion (45 per cent) of the transition placements from care was from residential care.

Young people stay in care for different lengths of time. Some young people are admitted to care on an emergency basis and stay in care for a relatively short period of time. Other young people remain in long-term care and for them this constitutes a large part of their life. Over 48 per cent (27) of young people were in care for more than five years. This compares to 11 per cent of the special school population who spent more then five years in care.

Table 4.9: Last Care Placement

Placement type	Number	Percentage
Health board residential unit	25	44.6
Foster care	13	23.2
Supported lodgings	7	12.5
Specialising/emergency care	7	12.5
Aftercare	2	3.6
Supervision at home	1	1.8
Family home	1	1.8
Total	56	100.0

Table 4.10: Length of Time Spent in Care

Time Period	Number	Percentage
Less than 6 months	4	7.1
6–11 months	5	8.9
1–2 years	11	19.6
2–5 years	9	16.2
5+	27	48.2
Total	56	100.0

The majority of care-leavers (59 per cent) in the study first entered care when they were between 11 and 17 years. This is a similar finding to that of Biehal *et al.* (1995) for Britain, who found that 62 per cent of the sample had entered care in their teenage years. It is important to note, however, that almost 21 per cent (12) entered care when they were less than one year old.

Table 4.11: Age on Entry to Care

Age	Number	Percentage
Less than 1 year	12	21.4
1–4 years	6	10.7
5–10 years	5	8.9
11–14 years	12	21.4
15–17 years	21	37.6
Total	56	100%

Almost 36 per cent (20) of young people had been admitted to care prior to their current admission. Twenty-eight per cent of young people (16) had been previously admitted to health board care. Seven per cent of young people (4) had previously been placed in a special school.

The largest percentage (55 per cent) of young people came into care under a voluntary agreement between the young person's parents and the health board.

Table 4.12: Legal Basis on Which Young People Came into Care

Legal Basis	Number	Percentage
Voluntary agreement between parents and health boards	31	55.4
Under an order issued by the court	21	37.5
Other	4	7.1
Total	56	100

For 7 per cent of the young people, there was no care order. In two of these cases the parents would not agree to sign a voluntary care order, and there was no information available on the remaining five cases. It is contrary to modern practice not to process a care order. Where necessary, care orders should be taken out by the health boards through the courts.

The following cases illustrate the diversity of precipitating factors associated with young people being admitted to health board care at a very young age. Factors include inability of parents to cope due to addiction and mental health problems:

Stephanie was born to a single mother. She never met her father. Her mother was a drug addict and lived intermittently in hostels for homeless women. Stephanie was placed in long-term foster care when she was a few months old.

Denise was born to a single mother. Her mother had a psychiatric condition and could not cope. When Denise was five months old she was placed in long-term foster care.

Sheila's mother left the maternity hospital when she was born and never returned to take her home. The health board tracked her mother, who had a problem with drink and led a chaotic lifestyle. Sheila was placed in long-term foster care.

Sean is the youngest of six children. His mother and father both had problems with alcohol. His mother left the family home when he was five years old. After being placed with his siblings in a placement that did not work out, Sean was later placed in a residential home.

The following examples illustrate the range of circumstances of young people who entered care when they were adolescents. Sexual abuse, physical abuse and inability to get along with partners of their parents were contributing factors:

Anne was born to a single mother. Her mother had a psychiatric condition and misused prescribed drugs. Anne felt rejected by her mother. It was also suspected that a neighbour sexually assaulted her. Anne displayed disruptive and violent behaviour and assaulted her mother on several occasions. At the age of 11, she was placed in a health board residential unit.

Mary's father sexually abused her. At the age of 15 years she developed an eating disorder and was hospitalised for an extended period of time. During this time she disclosed that her father had sexually abused her and she did not wish to return home, where her father was still residing.

When *Martin* was 12 years old and was playing in his friend's house, he refused to go home. He alleged that his father was physically violent to him. The friend's mother contacted the health board and he was taken into care.

Anna's mother died when she was seven. Her father married again and had a second family. Anna felt left out and ran away from home several times. She alleged physical abuse by her father and was taken into residential care at the age of 14. She has had little contact with her family since coming into care.

Contact and Access

The distance of the care placement from the young person's home is outlined below. Forty-six per cent were less than five miles away from their parent's home. Over 26 per cent (15), however, were over 40 miles from their home base. The parents of six of these young people had emigrated and in three cases their whereabouts were unknown. One young person, who lived in Letterkenny, Co. Donegal, was placed in a residential unit in Sligo, as there was no appropriate placement for her in the Donegal Community Care Area.

Table 4.13: Distance of Placement from Home

Distance	Number	Percentage
Under 1 mile	4	7.1
1–4 miles	22	39.3
5–19 miles	13	23.2
20–39 miles	2	3.6
More than 40 miles	15	26.8
Total	56	100.0

Gogarty (1995) and other authors emphasise the importance of contact with parents, siblings and extended kin. The separation from siblings, extended kin and community contacts can cause enormous grief and raises issues for the young person regarding his or her identify. Quality contact between young people in care and parents is important. One young person expressed the following:

> "When you are taken into care, you lose contact with the people you know and the area you know. When you leave care, you feel empty. You have no connections. You feel embarrassed. You don't know how to relate to the people around you or the place."

> "I did not know my family as I had grown up in a home. I met my family a couple of times a year. I never called my mother 'ma'. I called her by her name. When I went home it was like living with strangers."

> "It was weird to be back home. No one came in the morning to tell me to get out of bed, I kept asking permission to do things."

As Table 4.14 shows, over 41 per cent (23) of young people had contact less often than every six months or no contact with their parents. This figure is comparable to O'Higgins' (1996) figure of 44 per cent of children in care who had extremely poor or no contact with their parents or relatives, but it is much higher than Gallagher's (1995) figure of 21 per cent.

Table 4.14: Frequency of Contact between Parents and Young Person

Frequency	Number	Percentage
Weekly contact	16	28.6
Monthly contact	9	16.1
Every two months	4	7.1
Every six months	4	7.1
Less often than every six months	15	26.8
Never visit	8	14.3
Total	56	100

Contact took place in the parents' home (33 per cent), foster-carer's home (11 per cent) or health centre (5 per cent). Other places, such as residential homes, relatives' houses, cafés or restaurants, were also used for meetings between parents and young people. Eleven per cent of access visits were supervised.

Young people with no contact included young people in long-term foster care who were taken into care when the importance of a young person knowing their birth parents was not understood. It also included young people who had entered care in their teens as a result of difficulties with their family or as a result of being rejected by their family. Four of these young people left home and entered care after disclosing that a member of the family had sexually abused them. They would not return home, even for a visit.

Placement Moves

Many young people experience multiple admissions to care, and while in care multiple care placement moves. The disruption caused to young people by placement moves is well recognised in the international literature. Placement moves can further increase the sense of instability and uncertainly for the young person.

Thirty-two per cent (18) of young people did not have a placement move during their time in care, 36 per cent (20) had between two and four placement moves, 18 per cent (10) had between 5 and 10 placement moves and 13 per cent (7) had 10 or more placement moves. Three people had 40 or more placement moves. These three people, although they were in care under care orders, had no secure placement and from time to time were placed in temporary accommodation by the out-of-hours-service of the Eastern Health Board. Placement moves were not as significant for the special school population, with 9 per cent having four or more moves.

Misplacement

Social workers considered that just over one-third (34 per cent) of young people were misplaced. This compares to 23 per cent of the special school population. Many of the young people in health board care were considered misplaced, as they needed specialised care that was not available for them. Misplacement is a major factor in placement breakdown, which in turn causes severe disruption to and increased anxiety in the lives of young people.

Social Work Contact

While in care, 96 per cent (54) of young people were visited by a social worker. Seventy-five per cent (42) were visited monthly or more often. Seventy-one per cent (40) were referred to other services while in care. Services included counselling services, psychological services, psychiatric services, child guidance services, services for people with a learning disability and family therapy services.

Care Plans

Health board social workers are responsible for preparing care plans. A written care plan existed for 71 per cent (40) of the young people. For a further 16 per cent (9), there was an un-written care plan. Young people without a written care plan tended either to be in long-term care, where their placements were seen as stable, or to be relatively new cases where a review had not taken place.

Table 4.15: Issues Addressed in Care Plans

Issues	Number	Percentage
Family issues and relationships	44	78.5
Anger management	24	42.8
Developing a training/work plan	22	39.2
School attendance difficulties	16	28.5
Sexual abuse	10	17.8
Drug use	9	16.0
Alcohol use	4	7.1

N = 56

Given the key role that foster-carers and residential care workers play in supporting young people while they are in care, it is vital that they are aware of and familiar with the care plan.

The Irish Association of Care Workers (IACW) is of the opinion that there is a lot of ambiguity on what exactly constitutes a care plan. They note that a care plan can range from a few notes to a lengthy statement and formal agreement with the young person. It is the experience of the IACW that many of its members do not see care plans. In many cases where there is a care plan, the resources have not been put in place to ensure that it is carried through.

Frequent changeover of social workers can further frustrate this process. All of these factors can create tension between social workers and residential care workers. The consequences of this is that in many cases, rather than anticipating a crisis, the crisis is often allowed to emerge before there is an intervention from the social worker.

The Irish Foster Care Association (IFCA) makes a similar critique, maintaining that care plans are not being uniformly adhered to throughout health board areas.[6]

Experience of Care

Twenty young people who were in health board care were interviewed as part of the present research. While recognising their own personal difficulties, in general young people who were in residential homes all had positive memories of the placements:

> "I have great memories of the home. They taught me to communicate. Staff were great. We had great holidays. If you wanted clothes you could get them, not the best label, but maybe a cheaper label. I respect the staff. I often go back there and get a good welcome."

> "It was great. They help you to sort out your life and move ahead."

---

[6] Personal communication with researchers.

> "I now realise how much I miss the home. I appreciate how much staff did for me. There was always someone there to talk to. I see them very often."

Stability of staff and staff contact can mean a great deal to young people in care:

> "I had the same key-worker for six years. She was great. I trusted her and she understood me. I still see her. She is the one link that I have with the past."

Off the Streets, run by Focus Ireland, and Parkview, run by the Eastern Health Board, were praised by the young people:

> "Off the Streets is the best hostel. Staff communicate with you, the atmosphere is home-like. The food is not locked up and the fridge is open. There are weekly outings and activities. If you came in late you are grounded the next day, but at least you are let in. I had to leave, however, as I became pregnant. Parkview was also very good."

Young people had poor assessments of many of the other inner city emergency hostels. They were too structured and not tailored to individual needs:

> "It was very controlled. They wrote down the time that you went to sleep. If you made an arrangement with them to come in at 11 p.m. and if you arrived in at 11.05 p.m. you would not be let in and you were left on the streets."

Supported lodgings are suitable for young people who do not need a high level of support. They can be lonely and isolating for vulnerable young people who need a high level of support:

> "I did not like supported lodgings. There were too many kids in the house. I had to go outside to smoke. I had to share a room with another girl. I did not feel at home. There was no support there. Supported lodgings is meant to be more than lodgings."

Care leavers expressed an overwhelming sense of shame as a result of having been taken into care and many different strategies were adopted to conceal their identity:

"When people ask me where I am from, I tell them that I am from Ballymun, where my granny lives, as I do not want to have to explain that I have been in care all my life."

"I did not tell anyone that I was in care. I was paranoid about what people would think of me. How do you tell who you are to your boyfriend. I had to make up stories about the different schools I was in."

"If people asked where I was living, I would say that I was living with friends."

"The slag at school was that it was not my mother that I was living with."

"I tell people that my parents live abroad and that I had to stay in Ireland to finish my education."

Leaving Care

For 55 per cent of young people (31), their leaving care was precipitated by a placement breakdown. Placement breakdowns are caused by a variety of factors, such as personal identity issues, unresolved anger, a search for increased autonomy and, as stated above, misplacement. When a placement breaks down it can cause disruption to the lives of both the young person and the carer. By definition, the transition from care is not planned.

The vulnerability of many young women in care can lead to the breakdown of placements and to an unplanned transition from care. This is illustrated in the following example:

> *Mary* was taken into care when she was 14 years of age. Her mother had left the family home when she was a year old and her father was physically abusive. While in care, she was supported to address issues of rejection, abuse and parental alcohol addiction. Mary's placement broke down five times while she was in care. Mary needed a secure therapeutic placement where she would feel safe. While in care she met an older man, walked out of her placement and accompanied this man to England. Her whereabouts are unknown.

Only one-third (18) of young people returned home when they left care. This contrasts with the special school population where almost twice the percentage returned home.

Table 4.16: Destination of Young People on Leaving Care

Destination	Number	Percentage
Returned to family/relatives	18	32.1
Independent private rented sector	15	27.5
Remaining in present foster	7	12.3
Hostels	3	5.2
Supported aftercare/social housing	3	5.2
Homeless	2	3.5
Prison	1	1.7
Whereabouts unknown	7	12.5
N	56	100.0

Similar to the situation in special school, in many cases young people return home not because it is the best place for them, but because there is no appropriate alternative or because they are too vulnerable to survive in the private rented sector. This is illustrated by the following case:

> *Anne* does not know who her father is. She also feels rejected by her mother. Anne was placed in a health board adolescent unit, which could not respond to her needs. It was not sufficiently flexible and did not offer the in-depth therapeutic counselling she needed. While she was in the residential unit her mother did not allow her to visit home. Anne dabbles in drugs and the residential services were not able to engage her. Ideally she needed a placement in a high-support hostel with flexible structures, but this was not available. On leaving care at 17 years Anne moved into the private rented sector. But this was not an appropriate living arrangement for this young woman, as she was very vulnerable and could not survive living on her own. Anne eventually returned home to live with her mother.

Fifteen young people in the study went from a care placement to the private rented sector. In at least four cases, the move to the private rented sector was precipitated by the breakdown of a care placement. Young people who move to independent living are assisted by their social worker and residential care workers to find and move into their rented accommodation. They are also put in contact with the Community Welfare Service, which can provide household items for their new accommodation. The following case illustrates a planned transition from care to the private rented sector:

> *Catherine*'s father has a criminal background and is in and out of prison and is physically and emotionally abusive. Her mother left the family home when she was five years of age. Her mother became addicted to drugs and died of HIV. Catherine was first identified by the health board when she was brought to the casualty department of a city centre hospital suffering from an overdose of drugs. This was seen as a cry for help. She disclosed the physical abuse by her father and she was placed in residential care when she was 16. She did very well while in care and the residential care workers and social worker helped her to address personal issues. On leaving residential care, she moved into the private rented sector with the assistance of the residential care staff and the social worker. She will also be assisted by the outreach service of the residential care unit. Catherine's transition is seen as stable. Two years later, Catherine, who had a baby, was allocated a local authority flat. She had support from relatives and neighbours and was considered to have settled satisfactorily.

For others even though the placement looked hopeful, the placement in the long term did not work out:

> *Jim's* mother was a single teenage mother who could not cope with the pregnancy. He was born with a physical disability. He was placed in a residential unit at the age of one month. His mother never visited him and he did not know who his father was. When he was 15 years of age, the social worker traced his mother, who was now married with other children. Jim was angry. He felt rejected by the world. He

assaulted staff and had to leave his residential care placement. He was placed in two foster placements which also broke down. Jim dabbled in drugs and ended up homeless on the streets. Supported lodgings were arranged for him. Finally, with the assistance of his social worker, he moved to private rented accommodation. The social worker was unable to continue to give support to Jim because of the absence of an aftercare policy in the Community Care Area. In the absence of any other support he became involved in drugs, was evicted from his flat and two years later was homeless.

Seven young people who had a stable relationship with their foster-carers opted to remain living with them on reaching 18 years. The following cases illustrate:

Colm was placed in long-term foster care when he was three years of age. Several of his siblings were also placed in care as a result of his parents' inability to cope. Colm's placement was seen as a stable long-term placement. His journey through care was relatively smooth and he developed good relationships with his foster-carers. Making contact with his birth parents has not yet become an issue for him. Colm left school at 16 years of age and is pursuing a youth employment scheme. Two years after leaving care, Colm is in employment and living with his foster-carers.

Joan was placed in long-term foster care at the age of four. Her mother was addicted to drugs, led a chaotic lifestyle and did not make contact with Joan. By the age of 12, Joan was suffering from depression and had contracted glandular fever. She began inquiring about her mother and social workers helped to trace her mother, who was now drug-free. Joan also wants to trace her father, whom her mother has not been in contact with since Joan's birth. Joan's foster-carers find Joan's need to have contact with her natural parents difficult. When they became foster-carers 18 years ago, they did not anticipate that they would have to deal with these complex issues. Joan ideally needed counselling to help her to cope with these issues and the foster-carers needed to be helped to come to terms with the reality of her natural parents. The transition from care, however, was seen

as fairly stable. Two years later, Joan is living with her partner in the private rented sector and has a supportive relationship with her foster-carers.

These cases illustrate that young people at the age of 18 years
may not be ready to meet their natural parents. It is important
that an independent service is available for them at an older
age, which would help them to search for their natural parents
as recommended in section 1.3.

The two young people in the study who were homeless were
officially under the care of the health board until they reached
18. On reaching that age, they were discharged from the care
of the health board and remained homeless. While officially in
care, they were in contact with the out-of-hours service of the
EHB (see Chapter 5), but more often than not they slept rough.

4.3 FOLLOW-UP: SIX MONTHS AND TWO YEARS ON

Six months after leaving care 49 (87 per cent) of the original
population of 56 were tracked.

Two years after leaving care, 44 (79 per cent) of the original
population were tracked.

On leaving care residential care workers continue to work
with the young people. This is generally done outside the
regular workload and is often unpaid. Work undertaken can
include assisting the young person to settle into the new accommodation, helping the young person to budget and shop,
assistance in developing an education and work plan, and being available for the young person in times of emergencies.

All three health boards in their annual reviews of child care
services published under Section 8 of the *Child Care Act* acknowledge the importance of having leaving care services in
place. They all also acknowledge that aftercare facilities need
to be improved and increased significantly. Social work teams
operate different practices in relation to supporting care leavers. In some areas little or no support is given, while in other
areas intensive support can be provided. One social worker
explained:

"The manager needs to be interested in aftercare. When moving a young person into the private rented sector, I make a list of items that the young person will need, such as pots, cups, iron. These may be cut back due to lack of finance."

In some Community Care Areas which are made up of dispersed rural areas, there is an insufficient budget for travel, with the result that social workers, even if they are committed to keeping in touch with the young person, can only do so very infrequently.

Leaving care can be a terrifying experience for care leavers. In a residential care setting, there is a routine around meals and house meetings. There is always someone available for the young person to interact with. Leaving care for many of them means isolation and loneliness:

"Care was a horrible thing to be in. I wish I had died rather than going into care. I was nervous about leaving care and could not sleep at night. I was terrified of moving into the private rented sector. I did not think that I could cope."

"I did not feel ready to live on my own. Yet I did not want to share with strangers."

For many young people in long-term foster care, the decision to leave is less pressurising. It is more flexible, and many have the security of knowing they will be welcomed back to the foster home:

"I can't ever remember a decision being made about me leaving care when I was eighteen. I did not feel any pressure. I left for a while when I was nineteen years. The flat did not work out for me and I returned to my foster-carers. I feel like one of their own. I am included in everything, weddings, holidays and everything."

When young people get appropriate support it eases the fear and isolation, as the following illustrations show:

"I left the residential home and moved into a flat. I was only eighteen at the time. The home kept a room for me until I had settled in. They helped me to get the flat, which was nearby. My key-worker continued to see me for at least three hours a week. She helped me to budget and often came shopping with me. The staff in the residential home are now my friends and I drop in to see them often. They make me feel very welcome. It is great to have them. Just to know that they are there."

"The worker is very important to me. I have known her for many years. She is my link to the past. I would be hurt if I could not see her any more. I look forward to seeing her. I turn to her in a crisis. I would have done some harm to myself if I had not had her support. Young people leaving care should be given information on services they are entitled to and who to contact in a time of crisis. We need someone to turn to."

Living Arrangements

At the time of leaving care 18 of the young people went to live with their family or with relatives. Six months later, five of these had moved into other forms of accommodation and one had moved to England. In addition, five others, who had not originally gone to relatives, had moved back to their family/relatives, so that six months after leaving care there were 17 young people living at home or with relatives.

In the six-month period, five of the seven young people living with foster-carers had remained with their foster-carers. Foster-carers adopted one other young person. Two young people had moved, one to the private rented sector and one to his birth parents. Two years later, a third person moved to private rented accommodation. All of these three moves were planned and considered positive.

Table 4.17: Living Arrangements on Leaving Care, Six Months and Two Years Later

Destination	On Leaving Care (%)	6 Months On (%)	2 Years On (%)
Returned to family/ relatives	32.1	34.7	30.2
Independent private rented sector	23.2	24.5	18.6
Homeless	5.4	16.3	16.3
Foster family	12.5	10.3	9.3
Supported after-care/social housing	1.8	6.2	2.3
Probation hostel	1.8	2.0	0.0
Prison/detention	1.8	2.0	4.7
Local authority accommodation	0.0	2.0	7.0
Other	0.0	0.0	9.3
N	56	49	43

The importance of the health board providing adequate supports to foster-carers emerged throughout the study. The following cases illustrate where additional supports are needed:

> *John* was taken into foster care at two years of age. Both of his parents were unable to cope and he experienced physical violence and neglect from his parents. On reaching 18 years he had had no contact with his parents for seven years. John was clinically diagnosed as suffering from depression and related mental health problems. He was attending the psychiatric services and a rehabilitation training centre. Although the foster-carers were anxious that he remain with them, they needed additional supports from the health board to cope with John's mental health problems.

Like John, Tom's foster-carers also need additional supports to provide for the aftercare needs of Tom:

Tom suffered brain damage at birth and has a mental disability. He was fostered at the age of four. They taught him to walk and to gain control over his disability without any assistance or training from the health board. When he reached 18 years, a letter was sent from the health board stating that the foster care allowance and the social work intervention would stop. All allowances for treatment such as speech therapy and physiotherapy stopped. This coincided with Tom finishing school. "There was no care place or decision taken. We were not consulted. The board didn't even consider an alternative. On hindsight they should have consulted the family. We should have put their responsibility to them. There should be no cut-off age whilst the young person is living with the foster family and is dependent on the foster family. Foster-carers should not have to ask and fight for every pound for extra tuition, remedial teaching or hobbies."

Two years after leaving care, 43 young people were tracked. Thirty per cent (13) were living with relatives, 19 per cent (8) were living in the private rented sector, 9 per cent (4) were living in foster care, 7 per cent (3) in local authority accommodation and one young person was living in social housing.

Just over one-third (15) were living in difficult circumstances. Seven young people were homeless. Two young people were back in care, one young person was in a special school and one young person was in a secure residential unit run by the health board. Two young people were detained in secure psychiatric hospitals, two young people were in prison and one young person was in a drug treatment centre.

Moves

A high level of movement is an indication of instability. Of the 49 young people who were tracked, 37 per cent (18) of young people had not moved accommodation during the six-month period. Twenty-two per cent (11) had moved once, 16 per cent (8) of young people had moved twice and 24 per cent (12) of young people had moved three or more times.

Two years after leaving care, 20 per cent (9) of the young people tracked had not moved and 30 per cent (13) had moved more than five times. The remaining 50 per cent had moved between two and five times.

Education

Information was available on the age at which 46 of the 49 young people left school.

Table 4.18: Age on Leaving School

Age	Number	Percentage
15 or under	28	60.8
16	8	17.4
17+	10	21.8
Total	46	100

Sixty per cent left school at 15 years or younger. This was a similar percentage to the special school leavers who left school at 15 years of age.

As expected, almost 50 per cent had no qualifications on leaving education. A further 30 per cent had taken subjects in the Junior Certificate, and 10 per cent had taken the Leaving Certificate. Only three of the young people had progressed to third-level education. These three young people were all in long-term stable fostering arrangements. For those who remained in education, a higher percentage of those leaving the care of health boards (15 per cent) sat the Leaving Certificate or progressed to third-level education than those leaving the care of special schools (1 per cent).

Work

Twenty-four per cent (12) of the 49 young people tracked six months after leaving care were at work, 20 per cent (10) were on state-sponsored training courses and 39 per cent (19) were unemployed. Only 14 per cent (7) earned over £100 or more a week.

Two years after leaving care, information was available on the work situation of 38 young people. The percentage unemployed, at 24 per cent, had reduced significantly and the percentage at work, 34 per cent, had increased by 10 per cent. As with the special school population, this reflects the buoyant nature of the Irish economy. Numbers on training schemes had decreased, while numbers in home duties had increased. As with the special school population, many of these young people are in low-paid jobs and need to be supported to remain in their jobs and to pursue further training.

Three young people in further education were all in care with foster-carers.

Table 4.19: Work Status of Young People Six Months and Two Years After Leaving Care

Work Status	6 Months On (N)	%	2 Years On (N)	%
Unemployed	19	38.8	9	23.6
At work	12	24.4	13	34.2
On Youthreach/ Community Training Workshop course	10	20.4	5	13.2
At school	3	6.1	2	5.3
In further education	3	6.1	1	2.6
In prison/detention centre	1	2.1	1	2.6
Home duties	1	2.1	5	13.2
Other	0	0	2	5.3
Total	49	100	38	100.0

Networks of Support

Six months after leaving care 82 per cent (40) of the young people had contact with their families and 49 per cent (24) had some support from a family member. The main source of support the young person had is outlined below.

Table 4.20: Main Sources of Support Six Months After Leaving Care

Main Source of Support	Number	Percentage
Member of family	16	32.7
Member of foster family	8	16.3
Residential care worker	6	12.2
No support	5	10.2
Community Care social worker	4	8.2
Partner	3	6.1
Other	7	14.3
Total	49	100.0

Two years after leaving care, 73 per cent (32) had contact with a family member. Thirty-two per cent (14) had a good relationship and frequent contact with a family member, while 25 per cent (11) had little or no contact with the family.

A higher percentage of the special school population had better contact with their families with 47 per cent having good and frequent contact with their families, two years after leaving care and 15 per cent having little or no contact.

Two years after leaving care 57 per cent (25) had some support from a statutory agency or voluntary organisations. The social work service was the main service with which young people had contact, with 27 per cent (12) of young people having contact with social workers. Eighteen per cent (8) had intensive contact and four had contact approximately once a month with social workers.

Other supports being received included supports from a voluntary agency (16 per cent), residential unit (7 per cent) or a special youth project (5 per cent).

Ten young people (23 per cent) had given birth or were responsible for a birth of a child. Six of these young people were living with partners, three of whom were married to their partners.

Identity

Two years after leaving care 76 per cent of young people had unresolved relationship difficulties with family. Many of these difficulties related to issues concerning young peoples' identity. Relationship issues with birth parents emerged again and again throughout the research. It is particularly important for a young person who is in long-term care to establish links with his or her past and to get to know their family history. The following cases illustrate the type of challenges this can pose for young people:

> *Michael* was abandoned and left in a Mother and Baby home in the mid-1970s by his mother who was unmarried. His aunt fostered him. He was obliged to keep his identity hidden from his extended family. His mother, who was living in England, visited him intermittently. Michael could not understand why his mother would not talk to him about the fact that he was her son. Although Michael had been doing well at primary school, as a teenager he began to fall behind. Michael left school, and on reaching 17 years left his foster home and his home town and ended up homeless in Dublin. He was convicted of a drugs-related crime and entered a drug treatment centre. Two years after leaving care he was being detained in a secure psychiatric hospital.

Identity issues can be of particular concern to young Traveller children who are fostered by families who are not from the Travelling community. The foster placements of all four Traveller children who are part of the health board population broke down when they reached their teenage years. The following two cases illustrate:

> *Mary* came into care when she was less than one year. From an early age she was aware that she was from a Traveller background. Her foster care placement broke down when she was 11 and she was placed in a residential home. After several months a number of residential care placements broke down and she became homeless. She was anxious to get to know her family. Her aunt, who was a nomadic Traveller living in a caravan, agreed to have her live with her. Mary went to live with her aunt and had remained with her aunt when she was tracked two years after leaving care.

Noreen, who had a Traveller background, was placed in long-term foster care when she was two years of age. Her birth mother had a problem with alcohol and could not cope. The placement was seen as a semi-adoption. Noreen had no contact with her birth parents for seven years. Her mother then began to visit her intermittently. The relationship between her natural parents and foster-carers was difficult, as they were from different income and cultural backgrounds. Noreen was confused. When Noreen was 16 years of age, she left the home of her foster-carers and went to live with her boyfriend. The relationship with her boyfriend broke up after a few months. She was staying in a friend's house and the health board arranged to have her friend's family supported under the supported lodgings scheme. Two years on, Noreen had moved into the private rented sector.

Difficulties

Six months after leaving care, young people experienced a range of difficulties. Forty-seven per cent of young people (23) had difficulties in regard to accommodation. This decreased to 27 per cent (12) two years after leaving care. This compared to 32 per cent of the special school population who had accommodation difficulties six months after leaving care and 30 per cent who had difficulties two years after leaving care.

Two years after leaving care, 30 per cent (13) had insufficient money and 16 per cent of young people (7) had difficulties with reading and writing.

Two years after leaving care, 25 per cent (11) of young people needed assistance to develop an education and training plan and a work plan.

Issues relating to childhood sexual abuse concerned 23 per cent (10) young people.

Two years after leaving care 30 per cent (13) of young people were known to have an addiction problem. This is a lower percentage than for the special school population, where 43 per cent of young people had an addiction problem. Sixteen per cent of young people had taken part in a rehabilitation programme. As might be expected many young people were addicted to multiple substances. The main types of addictions which young people were coping with are listed below.

Table 4.21: Addictions of Young People Two Years After Leaving Care

Types of Substance	Number
Methadone	9
Glue	9
Opiates	7
Cannabis	4
Alcohol	3
Ecstasy/LSD	2
Prescribed medicine	2

N = 13

Two years after leaving care, 14 per cent (6) of young people were suspected of being involved in prostitution. This is a higher percentage than the 3 per cent for the special school population.

Two years after leaving care, other difficulties included unresolved relationship difficulties with family, which pertained for 75 per cent (33) of young people.

Homelessness

The number of young people who were homeless increased from two at the time of leaving care to eight six months later, comprising 16 per cent of the study population. Twice this number, i.e.16 or 33 per cent, had experienced some form of homelessness during the six month- period after leaving care.

The eight homeless young people comprised the two young people who had been homeless on leaving care, one young person who had been in the private rented sector, one young person who left the family home, and four young people who had been in supported lodgings or other insecure forms of accommodation.

Two years after leaving care 68 per cent (30) of the 44 young people who were tracked had experienced homeless. This demonstrates the severity of the problem of homelessness among the health board leaving-care population and the urgent need for an aftercare and resettlement service. In addition, three young people who were not tracked were known to have experienced homelessness. This contrasts with 33 per cent of the special school population who experienced homelessness two years after leaving the special school.

Table 4.22: *Young People Who Experienced Homelessness During Two Years*

Population	Known to have Experienced Homelessness Six Months after Leaving Care	Known to have Experienced Homelessness Two Years After Leaving Care
Special school population	30%	33%
Health board population	33%	68%

Twenty-four of the 30 homeless young people were from the Eastern Health Board region and six were from the North Eastern Health Board region. There was no young person from the North-Western Health Board region who was homeless.

Sixty-six per cent (24) of the leaving care population in the Eastern Health Board region were homeless during the two-year period after leaving care. The percentages of these young people who had contact with the out-of-hours service of the EHB and Focus Ireland in the two years after leaving care is outlined in Table 4.23.

Table 4.23: *Young People in the Eastern Health Board Population Region Who Experienced Homelessness*

Homelessness	Percentage
Contact with the out-of-hours service	75
Contact with Focus Ireland	54

N = 24

Three quarters (18) had contact with the out-of-hours service and 54 per cent (13) had contact with Focus Ireland. Nine young people had contact with both the out-of-hours service and Focus Ireland. This means that 92 per cent (22) of those who were homeless in the Eastern Health Board region had contact with either Focus Ireland and/or the out-of-hours service during the two-year period. This is a very high level of contact with service providers.

The staff of the Extension, a day activity centre and the settlement and support services assisted the 13 young people who had contact with Focus Ireland. Focus Ireland housing services housed six young people. Three were accommodated in Off the Streets, a short-term residential unit, and three young people were accommodated in a social housing project. Off the Streets is highly valued by social workers and by young people.

Although Off the Streets is highly valued by its residents, a number of difficulties were experienced. Difficulties included the short-term nature of the unit and the pressure to move on even though appropriate accommodation was not always available. Also, one young girl stated that she had to leave because she was pregnant.

The three people who were housed by the social housing projects had a history of multiple placement breakdowns. It was felt that the social housing project did not have sufficient supports for care leavers who are vulnerable and need intensive individualised supports, including therapeutic services and drug treatment services. They also felt that health board social workers did not provide adequate support. In relation to one care leaver, one staff member explained:

> "In comparison to residential care, housing here is relatively unstructured. You are given your own key and expected to live with minimal support. It was a culture shock for John. He needed a smaller environment with a much higher staff/tenant ratio. He had a lot of unresolved issues and he needed a key-worker to help him to resolve these."

In addition, the inner city was not considered suitable for young people who were vulnerable and at risk of becoming involved with drugs and prostitution.

Detention

Two years after leaving care, a total of 30 per cent (13) of health board care leavers had been charged with an offence and 32 per cent (14) had been arrested. The percentage that had been sentenced to prison had risen from 10 per cent (5) six months after leaving care to 25 per cent (11) two years after leaving care.

Table 4.24: Young People Who had Served a Prison Sentence Six Months and Two Years On

Population	% of Care Leavers Who had been to Prison During Six Months After Leaving Care	% of Care Leavers Who had been to Prison/Detention During Two Years After Leaving Care
Health board population	10	25
Special school population	39	65

In addition, two young people were detained in high secure psychiatric hospitals.

The percentage of health board care leavers in detention is lower than for young people leaving special schools. Special school leavers are more than two and a half times as likely to be imprisoned than health board care leavers.

Supports Needed

Two years after leaving care, social workers were of the opinion that 59 per cent (26) of young people needed additional supports. This compares to 75 per cent of special school leavers. Supports needed by health board care leavers include aftercare (34 per cent), a mentor service (16 per cent) and counselling (30 per cent).

One-fifth of care leavers needed supported accommodation. Many of the young people need accommodation where intensive supports are available. Projects providing accommodation need to have access to other specialist services, such as counselling and drug treatment services.

Other services needed included counselling for sexual abuse, community-based special youth projects and projects that would help young people to come to terms with their criminal behaviour. Two young people needed a service to meet the specific cultural needs of Travellers.

Table 4.25: Specialist Services Needed by Care Leavers Two Years After Leaving Care

Services Needed	Number	Percentage
Aftercare	15	34.1
Counselling (general)	13	29.5
Supported accommodation	9	20.4
Mentor service	7	15.9
Drug rehabilitation	4	9.1
Specialist youth project	5	11.4
Counselling for sexual abuse	3	6.8
Intensive probation supervision	2	4.5
Culturally appropriate Traveller service	2	4.5

N = 44

In the following chapter, we look at the young people who were out of home in the Eastern Health Board region who accessed the out-of-hours service.

5

The Crisis Intervention (Out-of-Hours) Service of the Eastern Health Board

"The gardai did not want us in the station. They told us to go and wait in Busarus *(bus station)*, but often they would not tell the social workers that we were there. I have waited there from 8 p.m. to 2 a.m. I was in school at the time. One of the teachers was great. If he knew that I had slept rough the night before, he would get me somewhere to sleep in the school for a few hours. Sometimes he would wait with me until the out-of-hours service opened." — Young woman out of home, aged 16 years

During the course of the study, it came to the attention of the researchers that a large number of young people presenting as homeless to the Crisis Intervention Service (known as the "out-of-hours" service), of the Eastern Health Board (EHB) had a history of being in care. Focus Ireland, which commissioned this research, was anxious to include the out-of-hours service in the research. Hence, a survey of the numbers, characteristics and presenting problems of young people seeking assistance of the out-of-hours service was undertaken over a five-day period during September 1997. To update the study, further documentary research was undertaken and interviews were held with staff members in February 2000.

5.1 THE OUT-OF-HOURS SERVICE

The EHB established the out-of-hours service in March 1992 in response to concerns raised regarding the situation of young people who were out of home in Dublin. The original objectives of the out-of-hours service were as follows:

- To provide for the needs of young people over the age of 12 who are in a crisis, when all other services were closed

- To prevent young people becoming "encultured" to street life

The out-of-hours service operates from 8 p.m. to 6 a.m., Monday to Friday and 9 a.m. to 5 p.m. and 8 p.m. to 6 a.m. on Saturdays, Sundays and public holidays. Six social workers, four team leaders and a social work manager staff the service.

How the Service Operates

Until December 1999, the only access route to the out-of-hours service was through a garda station. The gardai communicated with the ambulance control service when young people came looking for help. The out-of-hours social work team in turn communicated with the ambulance service to ascertain which garda stations had been contacted by young people. Members of the social work team travelled by taxi to the garda stations sometime after 8 p.m. and interviewed and assessed the young peoples' need for emergency accommodation. It was and still is often necessary to interview parents and family members to assess whether or not the young person can return home. This requires that social workers to travel to the home of the young person.

This system created difficulties for young people. Firstly, young people were forced to wait around until after 8 p.m. in the evening when they are assessed for a place. Secondly, young people had no satisfactory place to wait. When the garda stations were busy they were in the way. Thirdly, in many instances there were insufficient bed places to place the numbers of young people seeking accommodation.

There is now a second way of accessing the out-of-hours service. This is through a reception centre, on the north side of the quays on the Liffey, known as *Nightlight*, which opened in December 1999. The Salvation Army is contracted by the EHB to provide this service. The out-of-hours service can be accessed through *Nightlight* between 7.30 p.m. and 8 a.m. the following morning.

However, if the out-of-hours service has no bed to offer a homeless young person, the young person has to leave *Nightlight* at 2 a.m. Also, if a young person refers in later than 2 a.m. and there is no bed available the young person is not permitted to remain in *Nightlife* and in such cases the young person generally sleeps rough. Only young people who are known to the out-of-hours service and who have been assessed by a social worker can access the out-of-hours service through *Nightlight*. All other referrals come through the garda stations.

In any one night there are between 12 and 17 contacts made with the out-of-hours service and in any one week approximately 100 contacts are made. Just less than 60 per cent of young people access the service through *Nightlight*, with the remaining 40 per cent accessing it through the garda stations.[1]

Hostel Beds

Prior to January 1999, the out-of-hours service had seven emergency beds for young people seeking accommodation. An additional six places were made available in January 1999. Staff allocate places each night and on Friday nights places are allocated for the weekend. It is not necessary for young people who have been allocated a place to return to the service on Saturday and Sunday. If allocated a bed, the young person is given hot food and access to a bath and washing facilities for clothes.

Prior to January 1999, approximately one-third of all contacts made with the service were not accommodated (see survey below undertaken in September 1997). In other words over a five-day period, 23 of the 67 contacts were not placed. Docu-

---

[1] Documentary research from the out-of-hours service indicated that of the 218 referrals made in the first 14 days of February 2000, 41 per cent (89) came through the garda stations and 59 per cent (129) through *Nightlight*.

mentary research over a similar period (i.e. five days) in February 2000 indicates that of 72 contacts made, three contacts were not accommodated. The higher placement rate is the result of the additional places being made available.[2]

When There are No Beds

When there are not sufficient emergency beds available, staff are forced to make a decision about who gets an emergency bed. They have developed operational criteria for making these decisions. These include age, level of "streetwiseness" and vulnerability of the young person, and whether or not the contact is made prior to 10 p.m.

Given the shortage of beds, staff tend to give priority to younger people. During the survey period in September 1997, older teenagers found it difficult to get a bed. One 17-year-old who was in contact with the service five times over the five days of the survey was placed only once, and two other 17-year-olds that had contact four times were each placed only once. A 14-year-old girl, who was considered vulnerable and had consistent contact with the service, was placed each night. The out-of-hours social workers considered she needed to be assessed and placed in residential care. A 15-year-old boy who had contact on each of the five nights with the service was placed every second night. He first contacted the service in October 1996 and had made over 100 contacts. The out-of-hours social workers considered that his circumstances had seriously deteriorated over the year. He is now an intermittent drug user as a result of sleeping rough.

When no places were available for young people who approached the out-of-hours service, they generally spent the night on the streets. They slept rough in derelict houses, in the porches of public buildings and under bushes in public parks. During the summer time, some slept on the rooftops of high-rise flats. When they find a "regular sleeping spot" in public buildings, security firms generally move them on. For young people not placed, the social workers bought them hot food (burger

---

[2] Documentary research in the out-of-hours service.

and chips). By any standards this was a very limited response to the needs of young people who had nowhere to go.

Next Day

Young people using the out-of-hours service, whether they have been accommodated or not, are advised to make contact with the Community Care Team where they originally resided the following day. The out-of-hours staff fax the social work team and inform them that the young person has been in contact with the out-of-hours service.

If the young person is known to the social work service and has a Community Care Area social worker, the social worker may try to place the young person locally. If accommodation is not available in the local Community Care Area, the young person is advised to return to the reception centre or a garda station the following day when the out-of-hours service again commences.

Young people who have been assessed as eligible for a "homeless allowance" by the local social work and supplementary welfare service receive an allowance from their local supplementary welfare service. The allowance is currently £15 a week plus a free bus pass. Until recently the "homeless allowance" was administered by the Homeless Persons Unit located on the north side of the city.

Daytime Activities

During the daytime, many of the young people in the survey made contact with the *Extension*, a day activity centre for young people run by Focus Ireland and located in the south inner city. The *Extension* provides both a drop-in facility and structured programmes. The drop-in facility provides basic care facilities such as shower, food and laundry. It also provides an information service on flat finding and other legal or social welfare issues. Structured group activities are organised, such as group discussions, relaxation groups, outings to cinema, swimming or communal meals. More recently, Focus Ireland was contracted by the EHB to open the *Loft*, a facility specifically for young people less than 18 years of age. The *Loft* remains open until the young people can access the out-of-hours service through the Salvation Army reception centre, *Nightlight,* at 7.30 p.m.

Inadequate System

The increased number of beds available to the out-of-hours service, the presence of a reception centre run by the Salvation Army and the availability of the *Loft* run by Focus Ireland all signal an improvement in service provision. Nevertheless, the overall operation of services for young people out of home is still totally unsatisfactory, both from the point of view of social workers and young people.

The main problem is that there are simply not sufficient numbers of appropriate placements and support services for adolescents available at a local Community Care Area level. This has put pressure on the out-of-hours service, which was established as an emergency service in the city centre. Strengthening the service response in the city centre without providing adequate resources at the local area level attracts young people to the city centre whose needs should be dealt with at a local area level.

During the daytime young people are forced to trudge back and forth between their local area and the city centre. In their local area they report to their social worker, who becomes involved in a fruitless search for a bed at local area level, which is not available. Young people may also be required to be in the local area to receive supplementary welfare payments.

In the city centre they generally attend the *Loft,* which is on the south side of the Liffey, during the daytime. In the evening they make their way to *Nightlight* on the north side of the Liffey and from there are brought to an emergency bed for the night, if one is available, which they again leave the following morning.

If a short-term placement in an emergency hostel for young homeless people becomes available, young people are no longer forced to access an "emergency" bed each night.[3] However, many of these short-term placements break down due to

---

[3] There are five emergency hostels for young homeless people: Parkview, Le Froy House, Off the Streets, Sherrard House and Eccles Street.

the fact that they are not able to respond to the specialised needs of the young people.

Even if the placement does not break down many young people are forced to move out after a six-month period in compliance with the "length of stay" criteria which operates in many hostels. They again may have nowhere to move to, as there are insufficient long-term places, such as supported housing projects, for young people in their late teens. Almost inevitably the cycle of homelessness repeats itself.

5.2 STATISTICS

Numbers Using the Service

During 1992, there were 679 referrals to the service. Referrals increased from 679 in 1992 to 3,480 in 1997, which is an increase of over 400 per cent.

During 1998, 3,068 referrals were made to the out-of-hours service. As one would expect the largest per cent (94 per cent) of referrals were in the 12 to 17 age category, as this is the main category which the service cater for.

Table 5.1: Referrals to the Out-of-Hours Service, 1994–98

Age	1994	1995	1996	1997	1998
Less than 12 years	134	142	215	241	132
12 to 17 years	1,367	1,441	2,158	3,125	2,892
18+	53	28	128	103	44
Not known			26	11	
Total	1,554	1,611	2,527	3,480	3,068

The following table presents the numbers of young people who had contact with the service by Community Care Area (CCA) in 1998.

The highest percentages of referrals (22 per cent) came from CCA 7 (Dublin North Central) and CCA 6 (Dublin West with 17 per cent). Community Care Area 4 (Dublin South Central) had almost 18 per cent of the referrals and CCA 5 (Dublin South) had 11 per cent.

Table 5.2: Referrals to the Out-of-Hours Service by EHB Community Care Area, 1998

Referrals in 1998	Number	Percentage
Dún Laoghaire	123	4.0
Dublin South East	109	3.5
Dublin South Central	169	5.5
Dublin South West	541	17.6
Dublin West	354	11.5
Dublin North West	668	21.9
Dublin North Central	676	22.0
Dublin North	246	8.0
Kildare	24	0.8
Wicklow	106	3.4
Other	52	1.8
Total	3,068	100.0

5.3 FIVE-DAY SURVEY

In order to examine the level of contact which young people have with the out-of-hours service and the outcome for the young person, a survey was undertaken of young people in contact with the service over five days in September 1997.[4] Over the five days, 27 young people contacted the service.

The Community Care Area of the young people in contact with the out-of-hours service during the five-day study is outlined below.

---

[4] Young people contacting the service on a Friday night are placed for the weekend. A further ten contacts were made over the weekend. In addition, tenchildren under the age of 12 were referred to garda stations during the survey week. Of these ten, four were placed in hospitals and six were returned home.

Table 5.3: Community Care Area of Origin of Young Person

Community Care Area	Number of Young People
Dún Laoghaire	3
Dublin South East	2
Dublin South Central	2
Dublin South West	1
Dublin West	2
Dublin North West	5
Dublin North Central	3
Dublin North	3
Kildare	0
Wicklow	4
Outside EHB	2
Total	27

Seventy-eight per cent (21) of young people had an identifiable Community Care social worker.

Numbers in Contact

Twenty-seven separate young people between the ages of 12 and 18 years were in contact with the service, accounting for a total of 67 referrals.

Table 5.4: Contact Over Five-day Period

Number of Contacts	Number of Young People Having this Number of Contacts
5	3
4	5
3	3
2	7
1	9
Total	27

Table 5.5: How Long It Had Been Since the Young Person First Contacted Service

Number of Months	Number	Percentage
Less than 3	7	25.9
3 to 11	10	37.0
12 to 23	2	7.4
24 to 36	3	11.2
36+	5	18.5
Total	27	100.0

The majority of the young people who were in contact with the service had been in contact over a period of time. Thirty-seven per cent (10) had been in contact with the service between three months and eleven months and 37 per cent had contact with the service for over a year.

Given the length of contact with the service, it is not surprising that many young people had contact with the service on numerous occasions during the five-day survey. Over the five-day period, 18 young people (66 per cent) had more than one contact with the out-of-hours service and eight (30 per cent) had four or more contacts.

Table 5.6 shows the total number of contacts young people had with the service since their first contact.

Table 5.6: Number of Contacts

Number of Contacts	Number of Young People	Percentage
Less than 10	10	37.0
10 to less than 29	6	22.2
30 to less than 49	1	3.7
50 to less than 69	2	7.5
70 to less than 100	1	3.7
100+	7	25.9
Total	27	100.0

More than a quarter had contacted the service more than 100 times.

Outcome of Contact

The outcome of the 67 contacts made by the 27 young people in the five-day survey period is outlined in the table below.

Table 5.7: Outcome of Referrals

Outcome	Number	Percentage
Placed in emergency hostel	41	61.2
Returned to family, friends or relatives	3	4.5
Not placed	23	34.3
Total	67	100.0

Of the 67 contacts made during the five-day survey, 41 (61 per cent) were placed in emergency hostels and three returned to their family or relatives. This represents a 65 per cent placement rate. However, for 23 contacts (34 per cent), no emergency bed was available and the young person did not return to his/her family. These young people had no option but to remain on the streets all night. By any standards this is an appalling service offered to these young people.

5.4 PROFILE OF YOUNG PEOPLE

The age distribution and gender of the 27 young people in contact with the out-of-hours service over the five-day survey period are outlined below.

Table 5.8: Age of Young People

Age	Male	Female	Number	Percentage
14	4	3	7	25.9
15	5	2	7	25.9
16	4	0	4	14.9
17	5	4	9	33.3

Background

The majority of young people in contact with the service come from families where there are relationship difficulties, conflict and violence. Young people with a care background and a Traveller background are disproportionately represented among the young people using the out-of-hours service.

- 26 per cent (7) were Travellers

- 40 per cent (11) had spent time in care and had come to the service as a result of a breakdown in their care placement

- 81 per cent (22) were not at work or in school or training

- 44 per cent (12) had a serious drug problem

- 22 per cent (6) were known to be involved in prostitution

- The vast majority had slept rough intermittently.

The number of young people making contact with the service who had been sexually abused was not known by the out-of-hours social workers, but staff are of the opinion that a high number have experienced abuse.

5.5 YOUNG PEOPLE ON THE STREETS

The absence of emergency accommodation for young people who are out of home has been evident throughout the 1990s. Without sufficient beds, the practice in 1994 and 1995 was to refer young people to bed-and-breakfast accommodation. In 1994, 301 young people were referred to a B&B.

It was not, however, considered good practice to place young people in B&B accommodation. In January 1996, the IM-PACT trade union took a decision not to co-operate with that practice and an embargo on trade union members placing young people in a B&B was put into effect.

Given the shortage of beds and in the absence of bed-and-breakfast as an alternative, large numbers of young people were forced to sleep on the streets or in adult hostels.

Informed sources are of the opinion that, in addition to the young people who contact the service and are not accommodated, there is a significant group of young people who, as a result of persistent experience of not being accommodated, no longer approach the out-of-hours service for assistance. There are also young people who need emergency accommodation and will not contact the service because they are required to access it via the gardai who, they feel, are hostile to them. Other young people feel embarrassed if their friends know that they have nowhere to go and have to go to the gardai to get a bed.

The Association of Garda Sergeants and Inspectors (AGSI) have called on the government to provide adequate resources for young homeless children and to discontinue the practice of sending homeless children to garda stations to access the out-of-hours service (Cusack, 1997).

Children Under 12

The out-of-hours service was never intended to address the needs of children less than 12 years. Nevertheless, a significant proportion (7 per cent in 1997 and 4 per cent in 1998) of referrals to the service are children under 12 years. In the absence of a service for under-12-year-olds, these children remain the responsibility of the gardai. If the gardai cannot return the young children home, they place them in hospitals as "social admissions", if places are available. In 1998, 86 children were placed in five Dublin hospitals.[5] The average length of stay in any one hospital for these children ranged from one night to 52 nights. This by any standards constitutes neglect on the part of the state and a severe infringement of the rights of children, as hospital settings are inappropriate environments in which to meet the emotional and psychological needs of these children.

Street Culture

The additional emergency bed places and ancillary facilities provided by Focus Ireland and the Salvation Army to the out-of-hours service is a considerable improvement. Nonetheless, it is evident that these are not sufficient to meet the objectives of the

---

[5] *Dail Report*, 27 January 1999.

out-of-hours service — to link young people out of home back into mainstream Community Care services and thus prevent them from becoming "encultured" in street life. In the absence of adequate accommodation and adolescent services which can deal with the complex needs and challenging behaviour of these young people at Community Care Area level, a core group of young people are being left to drift in and out of homelessness. When on the streets, even for a short period of time, young people tend to lose contact with families, schools and support networks. Survival on the streets often requires young people to engage in begging, petty crime and prostitution.

Unprotected on the streets, vulnerable young people live in fear and danger and become prey to abuse. There is evidence of widespread sexual exploitation of young people by male adults.[6] Becoming the object of sexual gratification for male adults further lowers the self-esteem of the young person and creates distressing identity problems.

The current practice which allows young people to drift in and out of homelessness is contrary to the spirit of the *Child Care Act, 1991* and *the United Nations Convention on the Rights of the Child*, which aims to promote the interests of children and to protect them from all forms of abuse, including sexual abuse and exploitation. Current practice raises the question of how Section 5 of the Act should be interpreted in regard to the entitlements of young homeless people to accommodation. Given the ambiguity of Section 5, it is incumbent now on the Minister to clarify and define a policy in relation to the eligibility of homeless children to accommodation and support services.

These young people require secure, safe accommodation, intensive support and long-term counselling to help them to come to terms with a damaged childhood, the additional degradation and rejection by services and the exploitation they have endured while on the streets.

---

[6] Over one-fifth of the sample in the present study were known to be involved in prostitution. See also *Report of Working Party on Children in Prostitution*, Eastern Health Board, 1997.

A Forum on Youth Homelessness was established by the Eastern Health Board in early 1999 with the aim of developing an action plan for youth homelessness. Key statutory and voluntary organisations are represented on the Forum and money has been allocated in Budget 2000 for youth homelessness. Part of this money will be allocated to finance the action plan to be produced by the Forum. Also, in 1999 the Minister of State at the Department of Health and Children announced that a national strategy is to be developed to address youth homelessness, which will be published in the year 2000.

6

Young People Leaving
Probation Hostels

Lionsvilla Hostel and Sarsfield House, the two probation hostels located in the Eastern Health Board Region, participated in the study.

Between April 1997 and September 1997, seven males left the two probation hostels. Forms were completed for six young people on their circumstances on leaving the hostels, and a second form was filled out on their circumstances six months after they had left the hostel. The researchers wish to acknowledge the commitment and time given by staff to tracing the young people after they had left care. No young person was tracked two years after leaving the probation hostels. This was in part due to the changeover of staff in the Probation and Welfare Service responsible for probation hostels.

6.1 THE HOSTELS

Both Lionsvilla Hostel and Sarsfield House were established in 1972 and are administered jointly by the sponsoring body and the Probation and Welfare Service (see Table 6.1).

The hostels aim to provide the level of support and structure which will enable the young person to mature and acquire the necessary skills for coping and managing their lives. They provide residential accommodation for a period of between six months and two years for young males between the ages of 15 and 20 years who are considered to be at risk or who are homeless. In any one year, each hostel caters for between 30 and 40 young people.

Table 6.1: Probation Hostels in Eastern Health Board Region

Name of Hostel	Sponsored By	Age	Gender	Number Accommodated
Lionsvilla Probation Hostel, Chapelizod, Co. Dublin	Dublin Lions Club	15-18	Male	11
Sarsfield House, Ballyfermot, Dublin 10	Sons of Divine Providence	16-20	Male	18

Source: Probation and Welfare Service Report

Young people are referred to the hostels by the courts, prisons, Probation and Welfare Service and special schools for young offenders. Health boards also refer young people to Sarsfield House. They are not custodial facilities, but rather aim to provide support for young people who are motivated and committed to staying out of crime. While in the hostels all young people are required either to attend school, to undertake a training course or to be placed in employment. Hostels are also linked to counselling and therapy centres and drug clinics.

If there is a breach of the probation bond, for example if the young person is involved in drugs or commits a new offence, the young person is returned to court. The judge may negotiate new terms on which the young person may return to the hostel or he may be placed in another hostel. If this is not possible or the placement is not successful, the young person may be returned to a special school or prison. Young people resident in both hostels are randomly screened for drugs while in the hostels.

6.2 FINDINGS: YOUNG PEOPLE LEAVING PROBATION HOSTELS

Two of the six young people were 16 years of age and four were 17. Their socio-economic circumstances were similar to those leaving special schools.

Table 6.2: *Marital Status of Parents*

Marital Status	Number	Percentage
Married and living together	2	33.3
Married but living apart	3	50.0
Both parents deceased	1	16.7
Total	6	100.0

Two of the six young people had parents who were living to-gether. The parents of one young person were both deceased. Prior to his mother's death, she had no fixed abode and lived in hostels for homeless women.

Two fathers and none of the mothers were in full-time em-ployment. Three of the families were living in local authority housing, one in the private rented sector and one in owner-occupied accommodation. The home base of five of the six young people was in the Eastern Health Board region and one was in the South-Eastern Health Board region.

Table 6.3 illustrates that families of these young people ex-perience the same range of difficulties as families of young people in special schools. Domestic violence, relationship diffi-culties and addiction problems were prevalent.

Table 6.3: *Family Difficulties*

Difficulties	Number
Domestic violence	5
Relationship difficulties between young person and parent(s)	4
Relationship difficulties between young person and siblings	3
Alcohol addiction of parent(s)	3
Severe financial difficulties	2
Drug abuse by parent(s)	1
Mental health problems of parent(s)	1
Accommodation difficulties	1

N = 6

The young people themselves also had problems, as the next table shows. Disruptive behaviour and irregular school attendance feature high on the list of the difficulties experienced by the young people. It is also interesting to note that two of the young people had a mental handicap.

Table 6.4: Young People's Own Difficulties

Difficulties	Number
Displays socially disruptive behaviour	6
Is known to be involved in criminal activity	6
Has a criminal record	6
Has been an irregular school attender	5
Has a problem with drugs, solvents or glue	3
Has a problem with alcohol	3
Has delayed learning (due to irregular school attendance)	3
Has a learning difficulty (mental handicap)	2
Has physical ill health	1
Has been or is suspected of having been sexually abused	1

N = 6

Care History

Four of the young people had been admitted to care prior to their admission to the probation hostels. Two had been in the care both of the health board and a special school, and two had been in health board care only. Two had siblings who were in health board care.

One young person entered care when he was ten years old, three when they were 15 years and two when they were 16 years. Four young people had spent two years in care and two had spent between one and two years in care.

Current Admission

Four of the young people were on a probation bond and the Probation and Welfare Service directed their conditions of residence in the hostels. One young person was on "licence" from a special school and was also under the supervision of the Probation and Welfare Service. One young person was in the hostel on a voluntary care order, arranged by the health board.

Table 6.5: Current Admission to Care

Admission status	Number
Probation bond	4
Out on licence from a special school	1
Voluntary agreement with health board	1
Total	6

Table 6.6 shows the factors linked to the young person being taken into care.

Table 6.6: Factors Precipitating Being Taken into Care

Factors	Number
Criminal behaviour	5
Young person out of control	5
At risk of physical abuse	2
At risk of emotional abuse	2
At risk of physical neglect	2
Parents' misuse of alcohol	2
Young person abandoned	2
Siblings at risk of being sexually abused by young person	1
At risk of sexual abuse	1
Parental disharmony	1
Parents incapable of caring for young person	1

N = 6

The following profiles illustrate the range of social and economic factors that contributed to the young people being admitted to probation hostels:

> *Sean* is 16 years old. He is from a family of five children. Sean's family has a chaotic history. There is evidence of sexual, physical and emotional abuse. The health board is investigating the sexual abuse allegations. Sean is extremely angry and out of control and is considered to be a danger to other people. He had three charges for joy-riding and was placed in a probation hostel on a probation bond. While in the hostel he refused to attend counselling to deal with the abuse issues and workers in the hostel found it difficult to engage with him. Staff were of the opinion that Sean needed a secure therapeutic unit to help him to address the abuse issues and his anger. There was need for intervention in the family at a much earlier stage. One night, Sean failed to return to the hostel and on the same night he was charged with stealing and burning cars and was remanded to St. Patrick's institution. Sean's anger on this night coincided with family intervention by the health board in relation to allegations of sexual abuse. The fact that he remained crime-free until this episode was an achievement for him.

> *Fergal* is 16 years old. He has two siblings. His father died when he was very young. His mother was unable to cope and lived in chronic chaotic conditions. She ended up homeless, making her way from hostel to hostel. Fergal was placed in foster care when he was 12 years old. His foster home placement broke down when he was 15. He ended up living on the streets and was regularly in touch with the out-of-hours service of the EHB, which placed him in emergency care. He was also involved in crime, which included larceny and assault. When he was 16 years old, he was placed by the health board in a probation hostel. Fergal had counselling to address issues such as anger management, bereavement, rejection and crime. He found it difficult to deal with one-to-one counselling and he mistrusted adults. One night he absconded from the hostel and was brought before the court the following day for the theft of two cars. He was remanded for a week in St. Patrick's institution until accommodation was arranged with his uncle.

Niall, who has a learning disability, was referred on licence from Oberstown Boys' Centre to the probation hostel. He should have been identified and placed in special education at a young age, but this did not happen. His family lives in severe poverty and cannot cope. His father has left the family home and lives in England. It emerged during his placement that Niall was extremely volatile. He was angry at the absence of his father and felt rejected by him. His mother's new partner also rejected him and there was violence in their relationship. While in the hostel he was committed to St. Patrick's institution for an outstanding charge. He received a court sentence due to the seriousness of the charge, which related to the assault of a garda. It was difficult to address Niall's needs in an open hostel. He needed specialist services at a much younger age and should have been referred to services for people with learning disabilities.

Care Plans and Issues Addressed

Five of the six young people had care plans. It was impossible to develop a care plan for the sixth young person, due to his extreme chaotic behaviour. The following are the range of issues addressed by the young people while in the probation hostels.

Table 6.7: Issues Addressed by Young People While in Probation Hotels

Issues	Number
Criminal behaviour	5
Family issues and relationships	3
Anger management	2
School attendance	2
Drug use	2
Alcohol misuse	2
Developing training/work plan	2
Accommodation	2
Sexual abuse	1

N = 6

Management of Care

While in the probation hostels, four of the young people were referred for counselling. One young person was referred for drug screening/counselling.

Review meetings involving the Probation and Welfare staff and hostel staff took place fortnightly in Lionsvilla and monthly in Sarsfield House. Parents are invited to meetings in hostels on average every two months.

Contact is made by telephone with the Probation and Welfare Service located in the home base of the young person, in order to ensure that the local service is updated on the progress of the young person and to keep hostel staff informed on the circumstances of the family. This helps to inform the decision whether the young person returns home or takes up accommodation in the private rented sector on exiting care.

Review meetings were held to review the progress of five of the six young people while in the hostel. The sixth was only in the hostel for a short period. Parents attended one of the five reviews. In two cases, parents were not permitted to attend because of sexual abuse allegations in the family. The parents of one young person were not interested in attending and in one case both parents were deceased. For those parents who did not attend review meetings, the Probation and Welfare Service had contact with the families concerned and in the case where both parents were deceased, they had contact with an uncle.

Leaving Care

Four of the six young people surveyed were in the hostels for periods ranging from two to five months, one was there for ten months and the remaining young person was there for just over a year. Five of the young people left because their placements broke down, either because the young person breached the rules of the hostels or because of new convictions. The sixth young person was returned to court on an outstanding charge and was convicted of assaulting a garda.

Two of the young people were remanded to special schools and one young person was committed to a place of detention. A fourth young person was returned to the special school from which he had been referred. The two remaining young people were returned home.

6.3 FINDINGS: FOLLOW-UP SIX MONTHS ON

The Probation and Welfare Service filled out forms on the whereabouts of the young people six months after leaving the care of the probation hostels. One young person was in prison and one had absconded to England from an open prison. Two young people were living in their family home, one was living independently in the private rented sector and one lived in emergency hostels for people who are out of home. It was not possible to track the young person who had absconded to England.

On leaving the hostels, young people often have little support from family members or "significant others". For four of the five young people on whom there was information, relationships with their families were described by probation and welfare staff as "poor" and for the fifth as "fair". The support the young person was receiving from family members or significant others was described as "unsatisfactory" for four of the five young people.

Given the profile of disadvantage and adverse circumstances that the young people have to contend with, their work status was impressive. Two had regular work, one was in school studying for the Leaving Certificate, one was on a Youthreach training course and only one was unemployed.

The progress of three of the young people since leaving the hostel was assessed by the Probation and Welfare staff as "good" and the progress of two was assessed as "poor". Progress was assessed in terms of the young person's ability to develop a stable lifestyle. This involved staying out of crime or being involved in less serious crime, attending school, a training course, further education or work.

A brief profile is presented of the six young people six months after they had left care:

- One young person was returned home for breaching the rules of the hostel. Since returning home, his progress was assessed as "good". He is studying for his Leaving Certificate and is not suspected of being involved in crime.

- One young person was returned from the hostel to the special school from which he was referred, for breach of the rules of the hostel. Six months after leaving the hostel, he is living independently in the private rented sector, he is not suspected of being involved in crime and is in employment. His progress is assessed as "good".

- One young person was involved in stealing two motor cars and thus breached his probation bond. He was detained in a place of detention for a week and released on condition that he reside with his uncle and aunt. Six months later, he is leading a stable lifestyle living with his uncle and aunt and in employment. His progress is assessed as "good".

- One young person had a new charge on leaving the hostel and was committed to prison. Six months later he was with his family, who are homeless. He is residing in an emergency hostel and is unemployed. His progress is assessed as "poor".

- One young person who was charged with stealing and burning cars was sentenced to prison. He later returned to very unsatisfactory family circumstances. He returned to crime and again was sentenced to prison. Six months after leaving the hostel he is still in prison. Hostel staff are in contact with him and have let him know that there is a hostel place available for him on his release. His progress is assessed as "poor".

- One young person who assaulted a garda was sentenced to an "open" detention centre. He absconded to England and his whereabouts are unknown.

Success of Hostel Care

Young people residing in probation hostels come from difficult family circumstances. In turn, the young people can exhibit behavioural problems. The hostels give these young people an opportunity to address important issues. They support them to remain in work, school or a training course. They also refer them, where appropriate, to professional services such as counselling and support them to stay out of crime. However, given that hostels are open centres, residents are afforded a level of freedom which often results in involvement in anti-social activity.

Staff can find it difficult to engage the young people in reflecting on their difficult personal and family circumstances and many continue to engage in anti-social behaviour. However, their experience in the hostel can contribute in the medium to long term to positive outcomes: three of the six young people were making "good" progress six months after leaving the probation hostels.

There was no information on the circumstances of the six young people two years after leaving the hostels.

Appendix 1

Current Legislation

INTERNATIONAL LEGISLATION

UN Convention on the Rights of the Child

The United Nations Convention on the Rights of the Child was adopted by the United Nations General Assembly in November 1989 and ratified by the Irish government in 1992. This Convention emphasises the empowerment of young people and affirms their right to participate in decisions that affect their lives. The Convention also obliges governments to present periodic reports to the UN Committee on the Rights of the Child and to outline the extent to which the rights as guaranteed in the Convention are being adhered to.[1]

---

[1] Ireland presented its first national report to the United Nations Committee on the Rights of the Child in 1996 (Department of Foreign Affairs 1996). At the UN hearing on the report, the Minister of State for Foreign Affairs acknowledged that Irish child care policy was fragmented and piecemeal and that sufficient resources were not available to provide services for all children who need them (Ó Móráin, *The Irish Times*, 12 January 1998). The Children's Rights Alliance, which is a national umbrella body comprising non-governmental organisations, also produced a critique on the Irish government's implementation of the UN Convention (Kilkelly, 1997).

Legislation Affecting Health Board Care

Child Care Act, 1991

The *Child Care Act, 1991* represents a significant development in child care legislation in the Republic of Ireland. It places a firm responsibility on health boards to promote the welfare of children and to protect children. It strengthens the legal duties of health boards to support young people in their care and empowers them to prepare young people to leave care.

The *Child Care Act, 1991* espouses the principles of participation and empowerment of young people in decisions that affect their lives and is consistent with the principles underpinning the United Nations Declaration on the Rights of the Child. The Act, however, attempts to strike a balance between the needs of children and the rights and responsibilities of parents. It thus has to be read in the context of the Constitution of Ireland, which, in Articles 41 and 42, emphasises the importance of the family and of parental rights and obligations.

Under the *Child Care Act, 1991*, children and young people are taken into care under care orders. A range of new orders has been introduced. Section 13 empowers the district court to make an emergency care/protection order authorising the placement of a child in the care of the health board for up to eight days. Section 19 enables the court to make a supervision order authorising a health board to have a child visited at home to ensure that he or she is being cared for properly.

Section 12 gives the gardai powers to enter a house and remove the child without a warrant in cases of "immediate and serious risk". The gardai must deliver the child to the health board.

Section 75 amends the *School Attendance Act, 1926*, and provides health boards with a statutory basis to take children who are not attending school into care. However, young people can still be sent to industrial schools. These provisions greatly strengthen the powers of health boards and gardai to intervene quickly to protect children who are being abused and neglected.

Other provisions relating to children in care contained in the Act, together with the regulations[2] accompanying the Act, were introduced by the Department of Health in October 1995.

The legal definition of a "child" is now raised to 18 (Section 2).

A duty is imposed on health boards to promote the welfare of children in their area and to provide family support services (section 3). The underlying principle of the Act is that young people should be supported in their own home where possible and appropriate supports should be provided to allow them to do this. Health boards are thus challenged to provide community-based preventive services.

Children's homes and adolescent units are required to register and are subject to inspection (Section 61). Unregistered children's residential centres are prohibited (Section 60).

The health boards are required to develop care plans, to undertake regular reviews of children in their care and to facilitate access for people who have a *bona fide* interest in the child. They are required to encourage the participation of young people and birth parents in the development of care plans and at review meetings. Emphasis is placed on including the views of foster parents in the case of fostering, together with the views of the young person and birth parents.

A court may appoint independent legal representation for a child, separate from his or her parents (Section 25).

A young person in care is required to be visited by a social worker at least every three months in the first two years and every six months thereafter.

The Act distinguishes between children who are in need of care and protection and children who are homeless. Where a young person is homeless, the health board is obliged, under Section 5, to enquire into the child's circumstances, and if the board is satisfied that there is no accommodation available which the young person can reasonably occupy, the health

---

[2] Child Care (Placement of Children in Residential Care) Regulations, 1995; Child Care (Placement of Children in Foster Care) Regulations, 1995; Child Care (Placement of Children with Relatives Regulations), 1995.

board can make suitable accommodation available. A high court judgement has found that a health board must act in accordance with the requirement of section 3 "to promote the welfare" of the young person in its discharge of its functions under Section 5.

Section 45 empowers a health board to provide 'aftercare' support for children in their care. Assistance *may* be given in the following ways: visiting the young person at home, arranging for the completion of his or her education and arranging for hostel or other forms of accommodation by co-operating with housing authorities in planning accommodation. Assistance can be offered until the young person reaches the age of 21. This represents a significant extension of health board powers in relation to aftercare and enables health boards to take responsibility for the welfare of young people once they have left care. The Act makes it clear that preparation for leaving care should begin well before a young person ceases to be looked after and that preparation should commence two years prior to leaving care (regulation 5.v.).

Departmental Regulations and Guidelines

In 1996, the Department of Health introduced a set of regulations pertaining to residential care, Child Care (Standards in Children's Residential Centres) Regulations, 1996, and a Guide to Good Practice in Children's Residential Centres.

Under the *Child Care Act, 1991*, health boards are required to establish child care advisory committees to advise the health board on its functions. Under Section 8, health boards are obliged to systematically review the adequacy of services they provide, and to prepare a report annually on the adequacy of child care services in their areas. The functioning of these committees has been the subject of criticism by O'Doherty (1996).

JUVENILE JUSTICE LEGISLATION

In the Republic of Ireland a young offender is a person between the ages of seven and 16 years who has been found guilty by the courts.

Juvenile Diversion Programme

In 1963 the Garda Juvenile Liaison Officer (JLO) scheme was first introduced. It is now known as the Juvenile Diversion Programme. It is an alternative to court proceedings, which could result in a criminal record. The programme provides for the cautioning of juvenile offenders who are less than 18 years (subject to certain conditions). The main aim is crime prevention, which is achieved through the education of the young person regarding their responsibilities to themselves and others.

Probation and Welfare Service

The Probation and Welfare Service is responsible for the implementation and management of the community service orders scheme, which was instituted under the *Criminal Justice (Community Services) Act, 1983*. As an alternative to a prison sentence, the court may order a young person over 16 years of age to undertake a number of hours of service in the community.

The Probation and Welfare Service also funds hostels for young offenders. Local voluntary committees manage these hostels. There are probation hostels in Cork, Waterford, and two hostels in Dublin. They deal with young offenders between 14 and 18 years who are on probation or who are referred from courts or prisons. They provide a safe, secure, caring environment for young offenders who have a reasonable level of social competence and who do not have serious behavioural problems.

The Probation and Welfare Service has also established several community training workshops specifically for young offenders or young people at risk.

The Probation and Welfare Service provides a service to special schools. A full-time probation officer is assigned to each special school. The role of this officer is to liaise between the school management, the young person and his or her family, and the local Probation and Welfare Service who supervise the young person who is on release "on licence" from special schools.

Placement in Special Schools

Several factors govern the placement of young people in special schools:

- Criminal behaviour of the young person which, if committed by an adult, would warrant a fine or prison sentence

- Persistent non-attendance at school under the *School Attendance Act, 1926*

- Placement as a result of parents being unable to control the child.

Children Bill

The remaining sections of the *Children Act, 1908* are to be superseded by the *Children Bill, 1999* which was published in September 1999. The Department of Justice, Equality and Law reform has the main responsibility for the Bill.

This bill proposes raising of the age of criminal responsibility from seven to 12 years (Section 52). Under-age offenders will be referred to the health boards for assistance.

The definition of a child is raised to 18 years under the bill and section 156 abolishes the imprisonment of a young person under the age of 18.

Under this bill the Junior Liaison/Diversion Programme is to be put on a statutory basis, and diversion programmes are to be run by the gardai for young people who admit responsibility for an alleged offence (part iv). On agreement with the young person's parents, the junior liaison officer may convene a family welfare conference at a garda station, at which family members of both the victim and offender may be present. The purpose of the family conference is to give the offender an understanding of the consequences of his/her actions.

The minimum length of time a young person can currently be committed to a reformatory school is two years, with four years as a maximum. For a children's detention centre, under the bill, this is replaced by a maximum of three years (Section 149).

The court may make a care order or supervision order for a young person charged with an offence where it is considered appropriate that the young person be placed under the care of the health board (Section 78).

There are three areas in the bill which specifically relate to the role of health boards:

- The convening of family welfare conferences by the health board and putting them on a statutory basis (Section 7)

- The amendment of the *Child Care Act, 1991* and imposing a duty on a health board to apply for special care orders or interim orders in relation to a child in its area who is in need of special care and protection (Section 16)

- Providing for the establishment of a Special Residential Services Board to co-ordinate residential services for children detained in special schools and secure units.

Only minimal provision is made for aftercare in Section 208, which allows for the young person to be placed under the supervision of a probation and welfare officer on release from a children's detention centre.

The emphasis on diversionary programmes and in particular the provision to convene family conferences and to raise the age of criminal responsibility to ten is welcome.

Critics of the bill are unhappy with the lack of consultation with the staff of special schools, and with the replacement of the term "special school" with "detention centre", which has a punitive tone, out of keeping with the educational and rehabilitative approach of the special schools.

The lack of representation on the proposed new management boards of special schools for professionals working with
children, parents of children or organisations representing
children is critcised.

Also criticised is the absence of a co-ordinated response
across government departments to the needs of children and
the lack of a plan to locate the responsibility for children in one
government department.

There is need for a research unit to be established to examine the causes of juvenile crime and to recommend appropriate strategies for addressing juvenile crime.

Appendix 2

The Care System in Three Health Board Regions

EASTERN HEALTH BOARD SERVICES

The Eastern Health Board (EHB) region comprises counties Dublin, Kildare and Wicklow and is divided into ten Community Care Areas, eight in Dublin and one each in Kildare and Wicklow.[1] The population of the EHB region is approximately 1.3 million (36 per cent of the national population).

The numbers of young people in the care of the Eastern Health Board at any one time increased from 1,214 in 1996 to 1,554 in 1998.

In 1998, 70 per cent of care placements in the EHB region were foster care placements. Just less than 17 per cent of all foster children were placed with relatives and just less than 20 per cent were in residential care. The numbers in other accommodation, such as supported lodgings, account for an increasing number of placements, making up 113 in 1998.

---

[1] In November 1996, the Minister for Health announced that the EHB was to be replaced by a new Eastern Regional Health Authority. This Authority will be managed through three area health councils.

Table A2:1: Number of Young People in Care of EHB by Placement Type, 1998

Placement Type	Number	Percentage
Foster care	833	53.6
Foster care (relatives)	262	16.8
Residential care	297	19.1
Pre-adoptive placement	3	0.2
At home under supervisions	46	3.0
Other	113	7.3
Total	1,554	100.0

Source: Department of Health and Children

Foster Care

In each of the ten Community Care Areas, there are designated social workers that have responsibility for recruiting, assessing, training and supporting foster parents. A central team called the Fostering Resource Group supports this work. The recruitment of foster parents is failing to keep pace with demand for foster carers.[2]

The increase in numbers of children placed with relatives was notable as the 1990s progressed. In 1993, 37 young people were placed with relatives, by 1996 the number had increased to 179 and by 1998 the number increased to 262. The health board withholds one-third of the fostering allowance until relatives have been fully assessed. The Irish Foster Carers' Association is critical of this practice.

There is a lack of foster placements in the EHB region. In order to increase the supply, the EHB launched a major fostering campaign in 1996. This, however, yielded only 17 additional foster-carers. The low take-up was due in part to a delay in processing applications because of the workload of social work teams and the strain under which they operate. This delay in assessment caused some families to withdraw their applications.

---

[2] *Child Care and Family Support Services in 1996*, EHB

Emergency Carers Scheme

For some young people, placements in foster and residential care break down, and they are left without a care placement. A carers' scheme that provides carers with an enhanced fostering allowance and special training was established in 1989. The scheme aims to meet the needs of young people with difficult behavioural problems who are 14 years or older. The carer provides a temporary placement for the young person for up to four months, while their options of returning home or being placed in a long-term placement are being assessed. In 1994, a special social worker was appointed in each Community Care Area to recruit emergency carers.

Residential Care

There are approximately 54 residential centres, catering for 400 children and young people funded or directly run by the Eastern Health Board.[3] As in other health board areas, religious orders and voluntary organisations traditionally provided residential care. In fact right into the 1990s, the state only played a minimal role. In 1993, the Eastern Health Board directly managed only one residential children's home. By 1999, it managed 26 of the 54 centres. The remaining 28 centres are run by 17 organisations. The 54 centres include long-term, short-term, medium-term and emergency accommodation.

Residential care also includes two specialist centres for the Travelling community run by Traveller Families Care. Traveller Families Care is a voluntary organisation run by a management group and funded by the health board. It provides emergency and short-term residential accommodation for young Travellers. It also provides an aftercare service for Travellers who have left the residential centres.

There are two residential units which provide aftercare care. Aishlinn Aftercare Project, run by the health board, provides supported accommodation for four young women, a self-contained one-bedroom apartment for a mother and baby and

---

[3] Eastern Health Board, *A Strategic Plan for Residential Care in the Eastern Health Board Region*, December 1999.

an outreach service for young mothers.[4] Don Bosco Aftercare
Service offers a range of semi-independent supported accommodation in various locations in Dublin for young men.

Crosscare runs a non-residential aftercare project which
provides supportive and educational programmes. It provides
a non-residential aftercare facility for young boys between the
ages of 12 and 18 years, with the aim of reintroducing the
young people back into education and training. The project
also supports carers and parents of young people.

Publicity surrounding the issuing of judicial rulings in relation to the lack of high-support units has led to a number of new
initiatives on the part of the Eastern Health Board. In 1997,
Creag Aran residential unit was opened. It is located in County
Kildare and has places for six boys and girls aged between 10
to 12 years. It aims to provide a safe place for young children
who are experiencing difficulties living in the community. As
part of its programme, it provides educational and schools facilities for young people in its care.

There are two high-support units, Newtown House, County
Wicklow and Killinarden House, Palmerstown, Dublin, which
cater for 11 to 17-year-old children who have emotional and
behavioural difficulties. The young people are placed in the
units as a result of individual high court orders, which allows
the Eastern Health Board to restrict their liberty. The model of
work practice is not based on a juvenile justice model. The
units provide a therapeutic environment to respond to the
emotional and behavioural needs of the young people.

The 24-bed special care unit and a 24-bed high-support unit,
which were scheduled to be completed by the end of 1998, have
not yet been put in place. In the absence of sufficient secure
places, staff of security firms are caring for 17 young people in
the Eastern Health Board region at the cost of £2,000 each a
week.[5]

---

[4] Aishlinn also provides an outreach service to young women over the age of
16. It caters for a caseload of approximately 20 women ranging in age from 16
to 23. The young people are visited in their homes and club nights are also
available.

[5] "TD Critical of Arrangements of Children Needing Special Care", *Irish
Times,* 1 January 2000.

The Eastern Health Board estimates that the occupancy rate of residential care places is only 75 per cent. This is despite the fact that there is a severe difficulty getting placements for young people who need both long-term and emergency placements.[6] The numbers of young people being turned away from the out-of-hours service and young children being placed in hospitals as social admissions is also of increasing public concern.[7] The low occupancy rate can be attributed to the mismatch between the type of residential care places available and the demand for places.

Supported Lodgings

The supported lodgings scheme began in 1995 and is being provided under Section 5 of the *Child Care Act, 1991*, which requires health boards to make suitable emergency accommodation available for homeless young people. Like the emergency carers scheme, supported lodgings is a short-term emergency solution to the needs of adolescents for whom foster and residential care placements are not suitable or available.

The provider of supported lodgings is expected to provide good-quality accommodation and to provide the young person with a bedroom of his or her own. Character references are obtained and a garda check is undertaken on applicants. The positive aspects of this scheme are that young people are enabled to stay in their own localities and to stay in touch with their own network of friends. The success in recruiting families to participate in the supported lodgings scheme is attributed to the reasonable levels of payment that are made to families who provide this accommodation.[8]

Despite the development of the supported lodgings and emergency carers schemes in the EHB region, there is a major crisis resulting from the shortage of foster care placements and appropriate residential care placements. In some Community Care Areas, informed sources estimate that there are as many as 30 children assessed as needing care for whom placements

---

[6] *Child Care and Family Support Services, 1997.*

[7] See Chapter 4 and Chapter 5.

[8] Personal communication from the Irish Foster Care Association.

are not available. This resulted at the time of the study in staff in at least one Community Care Area operating restricted work practices and not processing any new cases. The crisis is also reflected in the fact that there are 2,400 cases on waiting lists in the region, awaiting the allocation of a social worker to undertake an assessment.[9]

NORTH-EASTERN HEALTH BOARD SERVICES

The North-Eastern Health Board (NEHB) region comprises three Community Care Areas: Cavan/Monaghan, Louth and Meath.

Table A2:2: Population of NEHB by Community Care Areas

Community Care Area	Population	Percentage
Cavan/Monaghan	104,169	20.7
Louth	92,163	18.5
Meath	305,703	60.9
Total	502,035	100.0

Source: *Review of Adequacy of Child Care and Family Support Services*, NEHB 1996

The number of young people in the care of the NEHB at any one time increased from 249 in 1992 to 370 in 1998.

The vast majority of young people placed in care in the NEHB region are in foster care (93 per cent), with residential care accounting for only 5 per cent of care placements.

---

[9] Personal communication from a senior staff member of the EHB. The Minister of State at the Department of Health and Children disputes this figure, stating that the correct figure is as low as 1,121 (Dáil Debates, 16 June 1998). The Irish Association of Social Workers, however, maintains that 2,400 is correct (Ó Móráin, 1998).

Table A2.3: Number of Young People in NEHB Care by Placement Type, 1998

Placement Type	Number	Percentage
Foster care	292	78.9
Foster care with relatives	52	14.1
Residential care	20	5.4
At home under supervision	3	0.8
Pre-adoptive placement	3	0.8
Total	370	100.0

Source: Department of Health and Children

In October 1995, the NEHB took over the residential services run by the Daughters of Charity in Drogheda, and its current services consist of the following:

- Two units in Drogheda. Valhalla, which is a mixed unit and provides care for eight young people, and Westcourt, which is a mixed unit and provides care for three males and three females

- Abbeygrove, Navan, which provides high support for three teenage girls with severe behavioural difficulties.

The board also has two aftercare facilities. One is a mixed-gender unit with three places for young people who are progressing from residential and foster care to independent living and the second is a one-bedroom flat which is attached to the residential unit and is used as a semi-independent living unit for older teenage girls.

The board recognises the need for a continuum of residential care options, including a crisis unit, a residential assessment unit, adolescent hostels, an intensive therapeutic facility, a residential psychiatric facility for children with psychiatric and emotional disorders and a unit for children with severe behavioural disorders.

The board also recognises that there are a small number of children who display an extreme level of aggressive and self-injurious behaviour, and who are not capable of engaging with the services. They need, the board suggests, "an intensive therapeutic environment in proper containment facilities".[10] During the period of the study (April–September 1997), two adolescent girls, a 16-year-old mother and her child and a 13-year-old boy with a learning disability were placed in Northern Ireland, in the absence of suitable services in the NEHB region.

The Meath Community Care Area has approved a post for an aftercare worker. The aftercare worker will support five to six young people who have left care and undertake preparatory work with young people who are leaving care. The person will also have a development role and will examine resources available for aftercare. Accommodation in the area is of particular concern and there is need to ensure that there is a continuum of accommodation options available.

NORTH-WESTERN HEALTH BOARD SERVICES

The North-Western Health Board (NWHB) region comprises counties Donegal, Sligo and Leitrim. The region is divided into two Community Care Areas as outlined in the table.

Table A2.4: NWHB Community Care Areas

Community Care Area	Population	Percentage
Donegal	127,000	61.1
Sligo/Leitrim	81,000	38.9
Total	208,000	100.0

Source: Information provided by the health board

On 31 December 1996, there were 196 young people in care in the NWHB. On the same date in 1998, there were 199 children in its care, 92 per cent (184) of whom were in foster care, 6 per cent in residential care and 2 per cent were at home under supervision. Forty of the 184 children in foster care were in foster care provided by relatives.

---

[10] *Review of Adequacy of Child Care and Family Support Services*, NEHB 1995.

Table A2.5: Placement Types in NWHB Area, December 1998

Type of Care	Number	Percentage
Foster care	144	72.4
Foster care with relatives	40	20.1
Residential care	12	6.0
At home under supervision	2	1.0
Pre-adoptive placement	1	0.5
Total	199	100.0

In the Sligo/Leitrim Community Care Area there is a small hostel, Teach Trasna, originally intended for homeless young people, run by a voluntary committee. This hostel caters for four to five young people, providing medium to long-term residential care and emergency care. It is fully funded by the health board.

There is also a children's home, Ballinode in Sligo, run directly by the NWHB, which caters for five to six young people. There is a flat attached to the home, which is used as an aftercare facility.

In 1997, the Castle Children's Home, Newtowncunninghan, Co. Donegal was opened. This was in response to the fact that there were no residential facilities in the Donegal Community Care Area. The Castle caters for children in need of residential care, children out of home and emergency placements. The building was formerly a Mother and Baby home. It is only a temporary home and it is planned to provide a purpose-built children's home in Letterkenny.

There is a need to develop the following facilities in the Donegal Community Care Area:

- A residential facility for young people for whom fostering is not suitable (for example, older teenagers and groups of siblings who cannot be catered for in any one foster family)

- An emergency hostel for young homeless people

- A residential facility with high levels of staffing for young people with challenging behaviour.

The large proportion of young people in foster care reflects the emphasis the board placed on developing foster care in the 1980s. In the Donegal Community Care Area, foster care is supported by a fostering team, and in the Sligo/Leitrim area, by a family and childcare team that specialises in fostering.

As in other health board regions, the number of people applying to become foster parents has decreased, and there is a serious shortage of long-term foster-carers for children who require a long-term family placement up to the age of 18 years.

An innovative project was developed by the NWHB in the Donegal Community Care Area in 1989 (Gogarty, 1995). It was estimated that approximately one-third of young people who were placed in care had experienced deep trauma in their lives and a treatment team was developed to respond to the needs

The team focuses on the attachment experiences of the young child and seeks to identify unresolved emotional difficulties resulting from trauma and to develop a programme for repairing grief and the sense of loss. The team seeks to help the child in his or her inner journey, working with sensory perceptions and emotions using sand, stories, painting and water. In order not to prejudice the trust between the child and worker, the team is not involved in abuse investigations. Work is also undertaken with the family of origin and with the foster family. The theoretical perspective underlying the team's work is outlined by Gogarty (1995). Although the programme has not been systematically evaluated there is evidence that it is making an important contribution to addressing the deep trauma experienced by many young people in care.

Health Boards' Views on Aftercare

Health boards recognise that young people leaving care are vulnerable and that the transition from care can be extremely difficult. In view of this, the boards see the need to put in place a range of support services for young people leaving care. In its latest report, the *Review of Adequacy of Child Care and Family Support Services 1996* (which each health board is obliged to publish under Section 8 of the *Child Care Act, 1991*), the NWHB recognised:

> The need to increase involvement with those who will be leaving care in the near future. These children have been identified as a high-risk group in terms of teenage pregnancy, involvement in crime and general difficulties.[11]

The NWHB also acknowledges that:

> Aftercare facilities require to be significantly improved, particularly for those children leaving long-term care...An additional community childcare worker is immediately required in each Community Care Area for this purpose.

The North-Eastern Health Board recognises that:

> Supported accommodation is often vital for a successful move away from care. Flexible living schemes such as independent furnished flatlets and halfway houses should complement residential care services. Closer co-operation needs to be developed between the statutory services and the voluntary agencies regarding the provision of accommodation and housing for those leaving residential care. The provision of outreach services is an essential adjunct to any programme of residential care to ensure that the necessary support is provided to facilitate the young person's transition to independent living.[12]

The Eastern Health Board states that:

> Young people who have been in care are at great risk of being homeless...This Review recommends that each group home be encouraged to develop intensive planning for aftercare with each young person in their care. The Eastern Health Board should consider a centralised training programme for managers of group homes to provide impetus to such an initiative.[13]

---

[11] *Review of Child Care and Family Support Services,* NWHB.

[12] *Review of Child Care and Family Support Services 1996*, NEHB.

[13] *Review of Adequacy of Child Care and Family Support Service in 1995*, EHB.

The EHB also acknowledges the need to give practical assistance to young people and information, that would include information on budgeting, accommodation and relationships.

Appendix 3

Logistic Regression Analysis

The statistical model used in the analysis is a binary response model, which postulates an underlying propensity to either succeed or fail in the transition from care. This can be estimated by using a combination of independent variables. This model — the logistic regression model — is widely used in applied research where behavioural responses fall into one of two mutually exclusive categories.

Coefficients for this model are calculated using *Maximum Likelihood (ML) estimation*, and identify the underlying causes of, or proxies for, the failure of a successful transition. Depending on the assumptions made about the distribution of the error term in the model, the model can be estimated either as a *probit* model or a *logit* model. In most practical applications, these two models yield identical results, although the logit model is often preferred as the estimated coefficients can be interpreted as "odds ratios".

Table A3.1: Variable Descriptions

Variable Name	Description
gender	Self-explanatory
f_ss	Special school/health board
rateprg	Perceived progress rating
nohome	Episodes of homelessness
addict	Suspected addiction problem
drugs2	Suspected drug abuse
alcoh2	Suspected alcohol abuse
es1	Currently in paid employment
es2	Currently studying
es3	Currently unemployed

es4	Currently in prison
arrest	Has been arrested
prost	Suspected involvement in prostitution
nummovs	Number of accommodation moves
travcomm	Member of Travelling community
s_needs	Special needs
abscond	Placement broke down
totmoves	Stability of care situation
famsupp	Family support since leaving care
support	Other support since leaving care
support2	Agency support, formal preparation
domestvi	Victim of domestic violence
sexabu	Victim of sexual abuse

Young People Leaving Care: Arrests

Dependent variable: **arrest**

Independent variables: **addict, alcoh2, drugs2, gender, f_ss, travcomm, s_needs, abscond, totmoves, famsupp, support (other), support2 (agency), domestvi, sexabu.**

Model type: **Logit**

Software used: **Stata v.5.0**

Initial results: **There are significant effects for gender, f_ss (special schools), abscond and totmoves, although the effect of alcoh2, drugs2 and travcommis are borderline significant.**

Logit Estimates   Number of obs = 134

                                  chi2(13) = 72.51

                                  Prob > chi2 = 0.0000

Log Likelihood = -55.412665   Pseudo R2 = 0.3955

---

arrest	Odds Ratio	Std. Err.	z	P>|z|	[95% Conf. Interval]	
alcoh2	3.817804	2.730119	1.873	0.061	.9399783	15.50635
drugs2	3.239293	1.99245	1.911	0.056	.970256	10.81469
gender	6.8247	6.502965	2.016	0.044	1.054411	44.17302
f_ss	36.58058	48.76405	2.700	0.007	2.682559	498.8292
travcomm	.1673452	.1558616	-1.919	0.055	.0269664	1.038493
s_needs	1.880752	1.100371	1.080	0.280	.5974749	5.920298

abscond	19.37642	22.69234	2.531	0.011	1.951659	192.3725
totmoves	1.560522	. 2708136	2.564	0.010	1.110585	2.192743
famsupp	.7694202	. 4522534	-0.446	0.656	.243131	2.434932
support	.4776587	. 2523192	-1.399	0.162	.1696202	1.34511
support2	.623128	. 2716187	- 1.085	0.278	.2651809	1.46424
domestvi	.9567619	. 4864253	- 0.087	0.931	.3532209	2.591561
sexabu	2.255931	1.462626	1.255	0.210	.6330703	8.038955

Final results: **drugs2 has a borderline significant effect on the probability of being arrested after leaving care, and travcomm is not significant. alcoh2, gender, f_ss, abscond and totmoves have significant effects.**

Logit Estimates   Number of obs = 134

chi2(7) = 66.11

Prob > chi2 = 0.0000

Log Likelihood = -58.615175   Pseudo R2 = 0.3606

arrest	Odds Ratio	Std. Err.	z	P>|z|	[95% Conf. Interval]	
alcoh2	**4.858868**	3.19579	2.403	0.016	1.338691	17.63559
drugs2	**2.867909**	1.5944	1.895	0.058	.9645933	8.526811
gender	**6.229474**	5.094693	2.237	0.025	1.254028	30.94535
f_ss	**23.25676**	24.79136	2.952	0.003	2.878598	187.8959
travcomm	.2827746	. 2417454	-1.477	**0.140**	.0529351	1.510556
abscond	**17.93891**	18.35891	2.821	0.005	2.4136	133.3296
totmoves	**1.560575**	.2461592	2.822	0.005	1.145564	2.125935

Young People Leaving Care: Prison

Dependent variable: **es4 (in prison)**
Independent variables: **addict, alcoh2, drugs2, gender, f_ss, travcomm, s_needs, abscond, totmoves, famsupp, support (other), support2 (agency), domestvi, sexabu.**
Model type: **Logit**
Software used: **Stata v.5.0**

Initial results: **gender does not discriminate between those in prison and not in prison, and is dropped (no females in prison). The only significant effect is for f_ss (special schools), although drugs2 is borderline significant. Results included for reference.**

Logit Estimates

Number of obs = 134
chi2(12) = 46.59
Prob > chi2 = 0.0000

Log Likelihood = -60.794874

Pseudo R2 = 0.2770

es4	Odds Ratio	Std. Err.	z	P>|z|	[95% Conf. Interval]	
alcoh2	1.17348	.6285785	0.299	0.765	.4107018	3.352931
drugs2	2.495274	1.384369	1.648	0.099	.8411527	7.402215
f_ss	99.80385	133.7097	3.436	0.001	7.223898	1378.869
travcomm	1.314354	1.055065	0.341	0.733	.2725405	6.3386
s_needs	1.710991	.9322861	0.986	0.324	.5880911	4.977956
abscond	1.89329	1.358939	0.889	0.374	.4637172	7.730024
totmoves	1.184382	.2336154	0.858	0.391	.8046277	1.743365
famsupp	.7046386	.3691088	-0.668	0.504	.2523969	1.967202
support	.7526351	.4313392	-0.496	0.620	.2447689	2.314263
support2	.7289953	.2898319	-0.795	0.427	.3344309	1.58907
domestvi	.7534828	.3569114	-0.598	0.550	.2977655	1.906656
sexabu	1.155149	.6895521	0.242	0.809	.3585283	3.721794

Final results: **Both drugs2 and f_ss have a significant effect on the probability of being in prison.**

Logit Estimates

Number of obs = 134

chi2(2) = 38.75

Prob > chi2 = 0.0000

Log Likelihood = -64.717693

Pseudo R2 = 0.2304

---

es4	Odds Ratio	Std. Err.	z	P>|z|	[95% Conf. Interval]	
drugs2	**2.852175**	1.274192	2.346	0.019	1.188248	6.846132
f_ss	**35.69459**	37.09218	3.440	0.001	4.65664	273.6101

Young People Leaving Care: Employment

Dependent variable: **es1 (at work)**

Independent variables: **addict, alcoh2, drugs2, gender, f_ss, travcomm, s_needs, abscond, totmoves, famsupp, support (other), support2 (agency), domestvi, sexabu.**

Model type: **Logit**

Software used: **Stata v.5.0**

Initial results: **travcomm dropped, as it does not discriminate between those in work and not in work (no Travellers at work). drugs2, f_ss, abscond, support2 (agency support and preparation) and sexabu are statistically significant. alcoh2, famsupp are borderline significant. Results included for reference.**

Logit Estimates

Number of obs = 134

chi2(12) = 35.37

Prob > chi2 = 0.0004

Log Likelihood = -54.795647

Pseudo R2 = 0.2440

esl	Odds Ratio	Std. Err.	z	P>|z|	[95% Conf. Interval]	
alcoh2	3.543774	2.693649	1.664	0.096	.7988431	15.72065
drugs2	.1100282	.0952853	-2.548	0.011	.0201538	.6006911
gender	2.050391	1.635528	0.900	0.368	.4294001	9.790646
f_ss	.1547147	.1209212	-2.388	0.017	.033439	.7158301
s_needs	1.328989	.7036773	0.537	0.591	.4707873	3.751615
abscond	.1494907	.1194557	-2.378	0.017	.03122	.7158071
totmoves	1.195794	.1938059	1.103	0.270	.8703617	1.642908
famsupp	3.311738	2.065919	1.920	0.055	.9751285	11.24735
support	1.504858	.69037	0.891	0.373	.6123465	3.698227
support2	2.470461	1.135245	1.968	0.049	1.003754	6.080351
domestvi	.4549837	.2417522	-1.482	0.138	.1605892	1.289067
sexabu	.2203914	.1582988	-2.106	0.035	.0539273	.9007006

Final results:

drugs2, f_ss, abscond, support2 and sexabu are statistically significant, famsupp and alcoh2 are borderline.

Logit Estimates

Number of obs = 134

chi2(7) = 29.69

Prob > chi2 = 0.0001

Log Likelihood = -57.634547

Pseudo R2 = 0.2048

esl	Odds Ratio	Std. Err.	z	P>|z|	[95% Conf. Interval]	
alcoh2	3.084225	2.135765	1.626	**0.104**	.7937906	11.98357
drugs2	**.1305161**	. 0979658	-2.713	0.007	.0299743	.5683015
f_ss	**.1506774**	.103319	-2.760	0.006	.0392991	.5777155
abscond	**.2000969**	. 483213	-2.171	0.030	.0468047	.8554438
famsupp	**2.781752**	1.585631	1.795	0.073	.9101726	8.501842
support2	**2.232035**	. 8826282	2.030	0.042	1.028264	4.845038
sexabu	**.2429302**	. 1549243	-2.219	0.027	.0696054	.8478516

Young People Leaving Care, Unemployment

Dependent variable: **es3 (unemployment)**

Independent variables: **addict, alcoh2, drugs2, gender, f_ss travcomm, s_needs, abscond, totmoves, famsupp, support (other), support2 (agency), domestvi, sexabu.**

Model type: **Logit**

Software used: **Stata v.5.0**

Initial results: **The only variables which were significant were drugs2 and gender, although sexabu was borderline. Results are included for reference.**

Logit Estimates

Number of obs = 134

chi2(13) = 23.28

Prob > chi2 = 0.0384

Log Likelihood = -46.541052

Pseudo R2 = 0.2001

es3	Odds Ratio	Std. Err.	z	P>|z|	[95% Conf. Interval]	
alcoh2	.6752262	.4468184	-0.593	0.553	.1845791	2.470109
drugs2	4.923763	3.360856	2.335	0.020	1.292067	18.7633
gender	8.574892	8.893996	2.072	0.038	1.122925	65.47969
f_ss	.5599661	.4589658	-0.707	0.479	.1123286	2.791472
travcomm	.7044833	.6856359	-0.360	0.719	.1045783	4.745693
s_needs	1.26374	.8117072	0.364	0.716	.3588609	4.450299
abscond	1.989753	1.322925	1.035	0.301	.5405827	7.323799
totmoves	1.090034	.1478649	0.636	0.525	.8355519	1.422024
famsupp	.6797477	.4140592	-0.634	0.526	.2059917	2.243085
support	1.593038	.920181	0.806	0.420	.513511	4.942
support2	.6365095	.2857135	-1.006	0.314	.2640714	1.534223
domestvi	1.409828	.782937	0.618	0.536	.4747424	4.186724
sexabu	2.995884	1.945432	1.690	0.091	.8390381	10.69715

Final results: **drugs2 and sexabu are statistically sig-
                                  nificant, gender is now non-significant.**

Logit Estimates   Number of obs = 134
                                         chi2(3) = 13.03
                                         Prob > chi2 = 0.0046
Log Likelihood = -51.667412   Pseudo R2 = 0.1119

----

es3	Odds Ratio	Std. Err.	z	P>|z|	[95% Conf. Interval]	
drugs2	**4.171058**	2.145091	2.777	0.005	1.522266	11.42883
gender	**3.810903**	3.296866	1.546	**0.122**	.6992643	20.76894
sexabu	**3.352167**	1.936924	2.093	0.036	1.080166	10.40305

Interpretation

Arrests

Whether a young person has been arrested since leaving care may be predicted from whether they are suspected of abusing alcohol (almost five times more likely to be arrested), whether they are suspected of abusing drugs (almost three times more likely), from their gender (men are more than six times more likely to be arrested), whether they were cared for at a special school (23 times more likely to be arrested), whether the care placement broke down (18 times more likely to be arrested) and from the stability of the placement (the odds of being arrested after leaving care increase by a factor of one and a half for each move from one care situation to another). The probability of being arrested after leaving care can be predicted with great accuracy using these variables; we can correctly classify 56 out of 76 (74 per cent approx.) of those who were arrested, and 42 out of 58 (72 per cent approx.) of those who were not.

Prison

Whether a young person is in prison can be predicted from whether or not they are suspected of abusing drugs (more than two and a half times more likely to be in prison) and whether they attended a special school (35 times more likely to be in prison). The latter odds ratio leads us to suspect a tautology, as special schools themselves have a custodial role for young people.

Employment

Whether a young person can find stable employment can be predicted from whether or not they are suspected of abusing drugs (those who do not abuse drugs are six or seven times more likely to be working), whether they attended a special school (those looked after by the health boards are more than six times more likely to be working), whether the care placement broke down (also has a strong negative effect), whether the young person received support from a statutory agency or formal preparation before leaving care (either of which double the odds of being in employment) and whether or not they are victims of sexual abuse (those who were not abused are four times more likely to be in employment). Family support increases the probability of employment, although this effect is only borderline significant in statistical terms.

Unemployment

Whether a young person is unemployed can be predicted from whether or not they are suspected of abusing drugs (more than four times more likely to be unemployed) and whether they are victims of sexual abuse (more than three times more likely to be unemployed).

Conclusion

It is important to stress that these interpretations have been phrased carefully to avoid implying direct causal relationships between the variables which we have discussed, and to allow for the possibility that association may be caused by a third commonly shared factor.

It will also be obvious, after even a cursory comparison of the odds ratios and significance levels in the model results, that many of the independent variables appear to have *substantively* very important effects which are nevertheless *statistically* not significant (This is the case where the P value is greater than 0.05). This is due to the low statistical power of the analyses, which in turn is a function of sample size. With a larger sample we would have the power to detect a much wider range of effects and to estimate much more precisely those which we have already discussed.

References

Biehal, Nina *et al.*, *Prepared for Leaving*, National Children's Bureau, London 1992.

Buckley, Helen *et al.*, *Child Protection Practices in Ireland: A Case Study*, Oak Tree Press, Dublin 1997.

Burke, Helen, *et al.*, *Youth and Justice,* Turoe Press, Dublin 1981.

Clarke, Michelle, *Lives in Care: Issues for Policy and Practice in Irish Residential Homes,* Mercy Congregation and the Children's Research Centre, Trinity College, Dublin 1998.

Collins, Michael L. and Catherine Kavanagh, "For Richer, For Poorer: The Changing Distribution of Household Income in Ireland, 1973–1994", in *Social Policy in Ireland: Principles, Practice and Problems*, Eds Sean Healy and Brigid Reynolds, Oak Tree Press, Dublin 1998.

Cullen, Mary, "Supporting the Child in Foster Care", *Irish Social Worker*, 15.1, Summer 1997.

Cusack, Jim, "Hungry Children Call on Gardai for Food and Shelter", in *Irish Times*, 27 March 1997.

Davy Economic Research, *The Irish Economic Report*, Dublin 1997.

Durcan, Gerry, "Secure Accommodation in the Child Care System: The Legal Background", in *Secure Accommodation in Child Care*, The Children's Center 1997.

Eastern Health Board, *Homeless Young People*, Unpublished Report 1987.

Eastern Health Board, *Report of Working Party on Children in Prostitution*, 1997.

Fahy-Bates, Brid, *Aspects of Childhood Deviancy: A Study of Young Offenders in Open Centres in the Republic of Ireland*, PhD Thesis, Department of Education, University College Dublin 1996.

Ferguson, Harry and Pat Kenny, "Introduction", *On Behalf of the Child: Child Welfare, Child Protection and the Child Care Act, 1991*, A&A Farmer, Dublin 1995.

Flynn A. *et al.*, "A Survey of Boys in St. Patrick's Institution: Project on Juvenile Delinquency", *The Irish Jurist*, 2, 1967.

Gallagher, Sheila, "Parents, Families and Access to Children in Care: The Implications of the *Child Care Act*", in Harry Ferguson and Pat Kenny (eds) *On Behalf of the Child: Child Welfare: Child Protection and the Child Care Act, 1991*, A&A Farmer, Dublin 1995.

Gilligan, Robbie, "Foster Care of Children in Ireland Issues and Challenges of the 1990s", Occasional Paper 2, Trinity College, Dublin 1990.

Goffman, Irving, *Asylums,* Penguin, 1971.

Gogarty, Helen, 'The Implications of the Child Care Act for Working with Children in Care", in Harry Ferguson and Pat Kenny (eds), *On Behalf of the Child: Child Welfare, Child Protection and the Child Care Act, 1991*, A. & A. Farmer, Dublin 1995.

Hart, Ian, "A Survey of Some Delinquent Boys in an Irish Industrial School and Reformatory", *Economic and Social Review, 7,* 1969/1970.

Hart, Ian, "The Social and Psychological Characteristics of Institutionalised Young Offenders in Ireland", *Administration*, 16, 1968.

Kelleher, Patricia, Carmel Kelleher and Monica O'Connor, *Making the Links: Towards an Integrated Strategy for the Elimination of Violence against Women in Intimate Relationships with Men,* Women's Aid 1995.

Kelleher, Patricia and Monica O'Connor, *Safety and Sanctions: Domestic Violence and the Enforcement of Law in Ireland*, Women's Aid, Dublin 1999.

Kennedy, Eileen, *Reformatory and Industrial Schools Systems Report* (also known as the Kennedy Report), Government Publications, Dublin 1970.

McCarthy, Patricia, *Focus on Residential Child Care in Ireland: 25 years since the Kennedy Report*, Focus Ireland 1996.

McCarthy, Patricia, *A Study of the Work Skills, Experience and Preference of Simon Community Residents*, Simon Community, Dublin 1988.

McGuinness, Catherine, *The Report of the Kilkenny Incest Investigation*, Government Publications, Dublin 1993.

McKay, Susan, *Sophia's Story*, Gill and Macmillan, Dublin 1998.

McWilliams, Anne, "New Developments in Alternative Family Care", *Irish Social Worker,* 15.1, Summer 1997.

O'Connor, Patricia, "Child Care Policy: A Provocative Analysis and Research Agenda", *Administration*, 40.3, 1992.

O'Doherty, C, "The Functioning of Child Care Advisory Committees — Is Partnership Possible?", *Irish Social Worker*, 14.1. 1996.

O'Gorman N. and J. Barnes, *Survey of Dublin Juvenile Delinquents*, An Post and Dublin Chamber of Commerce, Dublin 1991.

O'Higgins, Kathleen, *Disruption, Displacement, Discontinuity? Children in Care and Their Families in Ireland*, Avebury 1996.

O'Mahony, Paul *et al.,* "Some Family Characteristics of Irish Juvenile Offenders", *Economic and Social Review*, 17.1, 1985.

Ó Moráin, Padraig, "Government to Tell UN Committee Child Care Agencies cannot Cope", *The Irish Times* January 12th 1998.

O'Sullivan, Denis, "Social Definition in Child Care in the Irish Republic: Models of the Child and Child Care Intervention", *Economic and Social Review,* 10.3., 1979.

O'Sullivan, Eoin, "Juvenile Justice and the Regulation of the Poor: Restored to Virtue, to Society and to God", *Irish Criminal Law Journal*, 7, 1997.

Pinkerton, John, "Responding to the Needs of Young People Leaving State Care: Law, Practice and Policy in England and Northern Ireland", *Children and Youth Services Review*, 17, 5/6, 1995.

Pinkerton, John and Ross McCrea, *Meeting the Challenge? Young People Leaving the Care of the Social Services and Training Schools in*

Northern Ireland, Centre for Child Care Research, Department of Social Work, The Queen's University of Belfast, 1996.

Rafftery, Mary and Eoin O' Sullivan, *Suffer the Little Children: The Inside Story of Ireland's Industrial Schools,* New Island Books, Dublin 1999.

Richardson, Valerie, *Whose Children?* Family Studies Unit, University College Dublin 1985.

Robins, J., *The Lost Children*, Institute of Public Administration, Dublin 1980.

Stein, Mike and Kate Carey, *Leaving Care*, Basil Blackwell, Oxford 1986.

Stein, Mike, *What Works in Leaving Care?* Barnardos, Barkingside 1997.

Task Force on Child Care Service: Final Report, Government Publications, Dublin 1980.

Tutt, Norman, *Report of the Eastern Health Board/IMPACT Review on Child Care and Family Support Services*, 1997.

Whelan, Pat "The Irish Foster Care Association", *Irish Social Worker,* 15.1., Summer 1997.

Williams, James and Claire Colllins, *The Economic Status of School Leavers: 1994-1996: Results of the School Leavers Survey*, Department of Education, Dublin 1997.